# *The* ONION
## HARVEST COOKBOOK

# *The* ONION
## HARVEST COOKBOOK

Barbara Ciletti

**The Taunton Press**

## Taunton
### BOOKS & VIDEOS
*for fellow enthusiasts*

Text © 1998 by Barbara Ciletti
Illustration on p. 2 and photos by Boyd Hagen and
   Scott Phillips © 1998 by The Taunton Press, Inc.

Printed in the United States of America
10 9 8 7 6 5 4 3 2 1

The Taunton Press, Inc., 63 South Main Steet,
P.O. Box 5506, Newtown, CT 06470-5506
e-mail: tp@taunton.com

Distributed by Publishers Group West

Library of Congress Cataloging-in-Publication Data

Ciletti, Barbara J.
      The onion harvest cookbook / Barbara Ciletti.
          p.    cm.
      Includes bibliographical references and index.
      ISBN 1-56158-245-X
      1. Cookery (Onions).  2. Onions.  I. Title.
TX803.05C55   1998
641.6'525—dc21                              97-46765
                                              CIP

May your hands grow
warm and brown
from the glow of
morning sun,
And may the garden
within you
embrace each day
as the earth
hums with
gifts
for your
table.

# ACKNOWLEDGMENTS

Last year in Colorado, spring gave way to summer with little transition. June brought intense rain, July scalding heat, and August became the month of moody weather, which is not uncommon here. As the days passed, I planted my garden, watched portions of it wash away, and yielded once again to the teachings of nature. This cookbook came to life while my onions migrated, spaghetti squash sprawled, and oregano doubled in size. It was then that the friendship and support of so many people enabled the birth of this volume.

I am grateful to be a member of the Taunton team, as we brainstorm, joke, and sometimes knash our teeth in search of the perfect photo. Publisher Helen Albert somehow brings out thoughts and ideas that I don't see within me, and that facilitates creativity and a dedication to quality. Because of Cherilyn DeVries, even the challenges of deadlines gain levity through laughter. Thanks, Cherilyn, for your constant encouragement and for keeping us all on the same page, which was not an easy task. And many thanks to my editor Diane Sinitsky for her careful scrutiny of myriad details. This manuscript may not have had life without the careful guidance and even fortitude of Connie Welch, my teacher in the world of recipe assembly. The artful styling of Abby Dodge enabled those recipes to gain life under the camera lens.

Speaking of cameras, professional Tim Benko knows how to wield one. He never ceased to amaze me as he plied his trade. Seemingly bland white onions glowed like fresh water pearls, and cipollini blushed like a basket of baby roses under his careful eye.

My early years were filled with family and friends who lived with intensity and humor. However, memories of childhood harvests aren't so different from those of today. Eric, my husband of 22 years, gathers neighbors to our table with a gleam in his eye, and we join together to laugh, eat, and celebrate. Thanks to him, our house holds a bounty of tradition.

# CONTENTS

# INTRODUCTION

My family's vegetable garden in Washington, Pennsylvania, put food on the table, entertained our senses, and became the focal point for community festivity every fall. As a young child, I saw it as a source of freedom and discovery. I could wash my hands with dirt, ride my tricycle between corn rows, and listen to the insects all day.

At the far end of the property, the compost pile, clumps of buttercups, and apple trees made their way among the pumpkins. On one side, tall locusts and black raspberry bushes offered shade as well as the perfect food for summer pie. The grape arbor flanked yet another area with a colonnade of vines that burst forth with frosty white grapes in late summer. The arbor led to the chicken coop, which later became the garden shed and home for seeds, starter plants, the workbench, and more. The smell of garlic and onions permeated the air all year long. Bouquets of rocambole hung from the rafters, and small scallions, red onion sets, and garlic bulbs adorned the workbench. Outside on the other side of the shed were more fruit trees, the grape arbor belonging to our neighbor Mr. Emerick, and red raspberry bushes.

At the center of it all stood my father. This was his kingdom, and he reigned supreme. Each year I would follow him throughout the garden as he taught me to plant, fertilize, harvest, and use my senses. His methodical and meditative hands coaxed an immense yield from everything he touched, and he deliberately grew

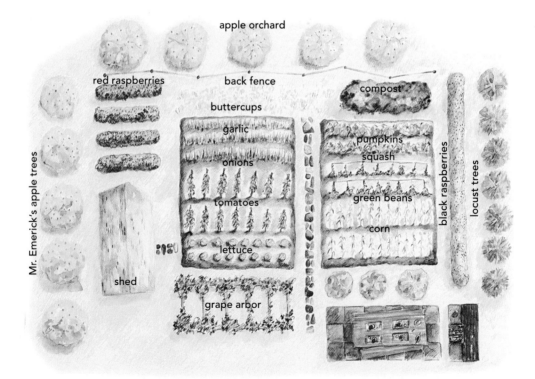

more food than our family of six could consume. He gave produce to our neighbors, relatives, Charlie the Eggman, Doc Sposata, the pastor at the church, and, of course, anyone who looked a little hungry, especially a friend who had little money and a large family.

We romanced the soil, and the earth reciprocated with a cornucopia of vegetables, onions, and the jewel of the kingdom—garlic. Once July passed to August, the air hummed with festivity. We harvested vegetables and planted more garlic for the following spring.

As baskets of food entered our kitchens, we washed, chopped, and sliced what seemed to be mountains of food for the pantry. I watched dozens of mason jars glisten with plum tomatoes, basil, and garlic. Pints of onions and peppers, green tomatoes with onions and dill, as well as plenty of pickled beets lined the shelves of our fruit cellar. As the days continued to usher forth more fresh produce for consumption, dinner expanded to include additional people at the table.

My mother was one of 14 children, and luckily for us, she loved to cook for a crowd. Our house was filled with people, their stories, and an aura of contentment. The harvest bred a sense of calm satisfaction as the hard work of the summer met its reward. And it was good.

As I began to experiment with more recipes from other countries, I realized that onions, garlic, and their cousins remain, without a doubt, major ingredients in cuisines all over the world. Their color, zest, and flavor add intrigue to food, as well as wonderfully authentic stories from cooks and kitchens on every continent. Regardless of origin, edible alliums rise from the earth and offer innumerable possibilities for the kitchen gardener.

This book provides stories, gardening techniques, and storage information about the onion family, with enough variety to please the newcomer as well as the more experienced kitchen gardener. The initial discussion encompasses bulb onions, garlic, shallots, leeks, bunching onions, and chives. Each offers an ancient contribution to the culinary and cultural history of the earth's peoples.

A garden just doesn't seem complete without the serpentine tops of Italian rocambole or the scent of scallions and chives. So the second section offers a guide for cultivating and harvesting exceptional allium varieties. Here you'll find growing tips, physical characteristics, flavor descriptions, and suggestions for short- and long-term use. Suggestions for harvesting from the garden and selecting produce are next, followed by information about how to handle and prepare onions to capture freshness and flavor.

The recipes combine research and experimentation to celebrate culinary contributions from a number of cultural traditions. Since folklore, anecdotes, and history make great kitchen companions, you'll find tales from family, friends, and fellow kitchen gardeners. After all, this book wouldn't be complete without the ingredients that make the harvest a festive time of year. I hope it always connects the gifts of the earth with people who seek guests for their tables.

# The Genus
## *Allium*

O nions, garlic, shallots, leeks, chives, and their cousins comprise both a wild and a domesticated tribe of bulbous plants that have inhabited the earth far longer than man can measure. While botanists, food historians, and archeologists have all ventured to pinpoint the time of onion genesis, there remains today no conclusive opinion about its exact time and place of birth. However, thanks to the comprehensive research of dedicated scientists, this diverse and somewhat rangy family does at least have its own tree:

Class: *Monocotyledonae*

Order: *Liliales*

Family: *Lilliaceae*

Genus: *Allium*

Cousin to asparagus and tulips, the ancient bulb onion has been prized for centuries. Whether red, purple, white, or yellow, its history is one of esteem, power, wealth, and health. In Europe, particularly during the Middle Ages, bulb onions were considered prized gifts for the bride and groom. In several cases, onions were literally used to pay the rent.

## BULB ONIONS

The emergence and later domestication of onions have left researchers scratching their heads for some time. While it's likely that the allium has origins in Asia, the desire to get specific about its birthplace has produced information that shows that onions could well have grown first in Persia and Pakistan. We know that onions grew in Chinese gardens as early as 5,000 years ago, and they appear in some of the oldest Vedic writings from India. One manuscript, purchased by the British Lieutenant

*Alliums grace the harvest with a medley of flavors and color. Onions, garlic, and shallots all share hues of rose, lavender, green, and gold.*

### ALLIUM SPECIES

| Species | Type | Origin |
| --- | --- | --- |
| Cepa | Bulb onions, shallots | Asia |
| Sativum | Garlic | Asia |
| Porrum | Leeks | Mediterranean |
| Fistulosum | Bunching onions | China |
| Schoenoprasm & Tuberosum | Chives | China, eastern Himalayas, Japan |

*This 19th-century drawing shows that onions were indeed a subject worthy of serious study. Doctors as well as cooks espoused the properties of cipollini, boiling onions, yellow globes, and hot varieties.*

Bower, was first found in ruins in Kashgonia. Its history of garlic was written around the 5th century but draws on the writings of Sus'ruta and Charoka, two ancient Indian physicians. In Egypt, onions can be traced back to 3500 B.C.

Renowned and respected food historian Waverly Root contends that onion culture cannot be relegated to one specific geographic spot of dirt. Rather, the onion found its way into the hearts and stomachs of man without lineage. In other words, since alliums apparently grew wild in various areas, they were probably eaten for several thousand years and domesticated simultaneously all over the world.

The onion, with its singular flavor and scent, made its way into a number of cultures, where its position extended beyond common dietary uses. The Egyptians, Greeks, and early Romans put it to great use in the kitchen, sports, romance, and daily life.

The onion symbolized eternity to the Egyptians, who buried onions along with their pharaohs. Ramses IV went to the other world with a single onion behind each of his eyelids, while literally heaps of onions were found around Tutankhamen's burial site. The Egyptians saw eternal life in the anatomy of this allium because of its circle-within-a-circle structure. Certainly, the onion must have been seen as the path to everlasting life.

The only Egyptians who were actually forbidden to eat the sacred allium were priests. Since onions often made one thirsty, the Egyptians were afraid that eating them would provoke a desire for too much wine, and drinking wine was not at all within the boundaries of acceptable priestly behavior.

While we can only guess, perhaps the pyramids would have never come to be were it not for onions. Around 450 B.C., the Greek author Herodotus traveled to Persia, Egypt, and other lands to record and accurately report eyewitness findings about the wars between Greece and other countries. He stood in awe of the pyramids, and once a translator relayed the story told by hieroglyphs, he came to understand just how much the pharaohs spent to erect their sacred tombs. The translator told Herodotus that the slaves who worked on the construction of the pyramids were fed a daily supply of radishes, onions, and garlic (the health benefits of these foods were recognized even then). The slaves worked around the clock—under grueling heat and amid exposure to disease—yet they maintained stamina and resisted illness. The cost of this rather primitive means of health insurance came to roughly 40 tons of silver, which on today's market exchanges to an amount of roughly 2 million U.S. dollars.

The Greeks not only cooked with onions but also used them to fortify athletes for the Olympic Games. In the final days before competition, athletes would consume pounds of onions, drink onion juice, and rub onions on their bodies. They assumed that if onions could build the immune system from within, then onions could inevitably build elasticity and muscle tone when rubbed onto the skin. During the 4th century B.C., Greek markets

*Onions grow prolifically in America and occupy an ancient seat in Native American diet, medicine, and history. The city of Chicago actually received its Indian name, "stinking onion," because the region was dense with wild onions.*

*After weeks of watering and care, the earth returns the efforts with a cornucopia of garden splendor. Freshly harvested produce seems to glow with color and energy. These golden Bedfordshires are no exception.*

abounded with onions, making them available for every home and every member of society.

The Romans ate onions regularly and carried pounds of them on journeys to their provinces in England and Germany. They loved onions and garlic so much that they made a concerted effort to spread their cultivation and use in the kitchen. In fact, the Romans' promotion of alliums remains one of the key factors in the spread of onions and garlic throughout Europe and eventually the world.

In the Middle Ages, Greek Emperor Nicephoros II once hosted an ambassador for the Holy Roman Emperor Otto the Great of Germany. Upon returning to Germany, the delegate bemoaned the Byzantine emperor's eating habits. For not only did Nicephoros consume a bounty of onions and garlic but he also washed down his meals with retsina, a delicious yet heavy and rather sweet wine. We'll never know what attacked the ambassador's sensibilities first—the onions, the lingering scent of garlic, which escapes the pores for days, or the retsina. It wasn't just the emperor's breath that filled the air; it was the wafting aroma of this entire being, which was only intensified by warm Aegean breezes. To add intensity to injury, onions and garlic were commonly thought to be the food of the common people. So Nicephoros' dietary plan not only exuded bad breath but also bad form! History doesn't indicate whether or not the German delegate returned to Greece for another visit. If he did, chances are that he didn't volunteer for the duty.

Centuries later, the first Pilgrims brought onions with them on the Mayflower. However, they found that their alliums were not the first to grow in the fields of America. A number of

*A legacy of flavor, lore, and cure has accompanied garlic throughout the world. Thankfully garlic travels well. The plant that most likely began in Asia now abounds all over the globe.*

strains of garlic, ramps, and tree onions grew throughout the various regions of North America and Mexico. We know that globe onions were a colonial favorite and were consumed raw, roasted, and pickled.

## GARLIC

Garlic offers an extensive array of history, legends, and lore. It seems that regardless of the story, the prevailing attributes of odor and health benefits prevail. We know that alliums, particularly garlic, found their way into Chinese medicine centuries before the birth of Christ and they endure today. And lusty Roman husbands held garlic in especially high

### A TULIP BY ANY OTHER NAME

According to legend, the prophet Abraham had convinced the Sumerian people of the city of Ur to plant garlic among their tulips in order to produce garlic with a sweeter flavor and aroma. The Sumerians followed his advice, only to harvest tulips that smelled like garlic. Their entire tulip industry was destroyed, and Abraham fled in record time.

## VACUUM BRAND GARLIC

Is a powder made from the very best selected garlic. The garlic is prepared, evaporated and dried by a process of our own which saves the free garlic oil and natural flavor. It is then powdered. When used in this powdered form to flavor sausage or any article of food, it is so thoroughly distributed in minute particles that it produces a more uniform and delicate flavor than can be obtained by using fresh garlic.

The use of fresh garlic requires considerable labor of a disagreeable character, and also taints the fingers and utensils with a lasting and offensive odor. Vacuum Brand Garlic enables one to use this delicious and desirable flavor without the many disagreeable objections to the use of fresh garlic.

**Vacuum Brand Garlic** will keep in any climate; it never deteriorates in strength or flavor; it never spoils; it is always ready for immediate use and is uniform in strength and flavor.

For flavoring Salami or Garlic Sausage and other foods, Vacuum Brand Garlic is much better than fresh garlic, because it does not undergo fermentation nor produce gases like fresh garlic.

**WE GUARANTEE** that Vacuum Brand Garlic Compound complies with the regulations under all the Pure Food Laws, and our guarantee under the National Pure Food Law, with serial number, is affixed to every package. It is made with the utmost regard to purity and cleanliness and contains no harmful or deleterious ingredients of any kind,

### PRICE LIST

| | | |
|---|---|---|
| One pound cans | per pound, | 35c |
| Five pound cans | " " | 30c |
| Ten pound cans | " " | 29c |
| Twenty-five pound cans | " " | 28c |
| Fifty pound cans | " " | 27c |
| One hundred pound cans | " " | 26c |
| Barrel lots | " " | 25c |

*Garlic took on a new dimension with processes that allowed for dehydration and packing. Companies such as B. Heller began to offer garlic in cans from 1 to 100 pounds. Making sausage and other cured meats became easier and less time consuming because of that vacuum-packed can.*

esteem, as they chewed it raw when returning home from the brothel. It never failed to mask their whereabouts—probably because their wives wouldn't go near them!

The use of garlic more than likely originated in China, then spread to Greece and Egypt. Later on, the explorer Marco Polo found the people of the Yunnan province in China eating raw meat covered with garlic sauce. It was there as well as in other places that the preservation qualities of garlic became so widely used. The powerful function of garlic when used as a spice ensured a war against microbes residing in raw flesh, and it provided an important safeguard against the very painful side effects of meat poisoning. When rubbed and covered with fresh pungent garlic, meat lasted at least twice as long as it normally would have.

Once garlic journeyed into European countries, it became an essential ingredient in the kitchen and in the medicine chest. In the 17th century, astrologer and physician Nicholas Culpepper wrote *The Family Herbal*, a compendium of previously unwritten or unknown information about the world of herbal identification and cures. Culpepper extolled the virtues of garlic, offering it as a cure for the plague, ulcers, and even bites from mad dogs. However, he also shared the importance of garlic as an elixir and contributor to overall good health. The use of garlic as a builder for the immune system and killer of harmful bacteria had long been appreciated in Asia and the Middle East. Now Europe had not only an organized and written record but also an illustrated collection of garlic and its abilities. Culpepper claimed that garlic killed worms in children, cleared the head, alleviated the effects of depression, and generally kept man out of a state of lethargy. People took his advice and found that it worked. It's

## GONE FISHIN'

The year was 1918 or 1919. The wood-frame schoolhouse held grades one through six, with a capacity for roughly 30 children. The day was a hot one in June, with 90% humidity and temperatures hovering around 92°F. Len and Joe Ciletti were in their seats at 9 A.M., but their minds were on to other adventures—namely picking berries and cooling off at the local swimming hole. Len and Joe, along with a number of other students, wore garlic around their necks. That year had been a bad one for the croup, and many of the poorer families believed that the garlic would fend off illness and a doctor bill.

The Sister of Mercy in charge of the children's education turned to write on the chalkboard. Joe slipped the garlic from his neck, removed two cloves, smashed them on the floor with his shoe, then moved his desk to cover the garlic. Within a half hour, the room was stifling with heat and nearly unbearable with the heavy aroma of garlic. Class was dismissed. Joe and Len went swimming, and the good sister never did find out who did the deed.

not surprising that it did, since years of research, experimentation, and study accumulated before this physician created this handbook.

Long before Europeans landed on the shores of North America, Native Americans were using garlic and onions as medicine. They roasted onions until soft, extracted the liquid, and mixed it with honey. This concoction was used for combating congestion, extracting worms, and healing open wounds. The homemade syrup worked internally and externally to cure a number of ills and to maintain good health, especially during unforgiving winters. Of course, folk medicine offers stories of wearing garlic around your neck to ward off disagreeable germs that cause colds and bronchitis. Since garlic can kill germs, it's likely that the fumes have some effect. I don't think that its abilities to frighten vampires has ever been proven, though.

As immigrants made their way to the shores of North America, the use of garlic and its cousins built a huge cultural and culinary legacy that virtually exploded later on during the

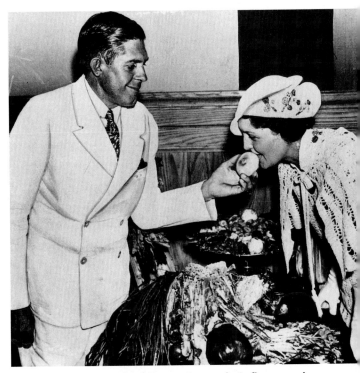

*While all onions are high in nutrients, their flavor and odor vary. Getting control of the smell may be in part due to Dr. Lloyd Shanklin (left). In 1935, he created an odorless onion by successfully crossbreeding specimens to eliminate the sulfur content.*

20th century. As the Germans planted their potatoes in American soil, they also planted onions and garlic. During the early years of America, immigrants owned little from their past lives, except for a few clothes, food, seeds, and tools for the beginning of a new life. They shared what they had, including their crops. Thus garlic spread from one community to another. It fed cowboys and ranchers and staved off disease for the settlers on many a wagon train. As America began to boom, Chinese, African-American, Italian, and Irish immigrants ate onions, garlic, ramps, and leeks on a regular basis. Their recipes for soups, stews, and cure-alls have been passed from one generation of Americans to another.

*Shallots grew wild before being domesticated for the kitchen. They, along with other alliums, became a vital part of medicine as well as cuisine in Asia for thousands of years.*

Today, Americans have completely adopted garlic as part of their cultural and culinary heritage. Between 1975 and 1994, garlic production in the United States nearly doubled. The United States now grows at least 500 million pounds of garlic every year and imports more than 100 million pounds of the "stinking rose" from countries such as Spain, Chile, China, Mexico, and Argentina.

Garlic lovers have developed their very own culture with films, books, recipes, and folklore all celebrating this allium that began wild so many centuries ago in the hills of Asia. What appears to be a simple-looking bulb has effectively lowered blood pressure and cleansed the body for thousands of years. However, I think that garlic in the kitchen provides the best romance of all. Whether raw or cooked, its aroma and flavor provoke a desire for more. It enchants, delights, and seduces the senses. As I began to use garlic more and more, I realized that just about any recipe gained a special quality when blessed with a little garlic. Now, I add it to nearly everything I create in the kitchen. Well, almost everything—garlic just doesn't make a very good chocolate chip cookie.

## OTHER ALLIUMS

While bulb onions and garlic are probably the most popular alliums, the family includes shallots, leeks, bunching onions, and chives. Like their bulb onion cousins, shallots originated in Asia and remain a popular food there today. The shallot made its way to the Middle East, where it received the name "Ascalon" from the Israelites. The shallot became a culinary favorite there not only because of its mild taste and creamy texture but also because it could be grown in abundance. Because this allium grows in clusters underground, it offered plenty of easily grown food for all members of that society, regardless of standing. The shallot didn't get to Europe until about the 12th century, when the Crusaders returned home with bags of this bulb on horseback.

The leek may be the queen of the French kitchen today, but it really gained its reputation in early Rome. In fact, the emperor Nero was nicknamed "the leek eater." He apparently ate more leeks than garlic or onions in hopes of sweetening his singing voice. The Roman military were equally fond of the tender, sweet flavor of leeks, as they carried leeks to Europe amid their conquests. From there, leeks grew and thrived in the British Isles, where they were used prolifically in the kitchen and stood as a symbol of the Celtic people. And as legend has it, the Welsh wore leeks on their hats during a Welsh-Saxon battle in A.D. 640 and used the leek as their national emblem.

Bunching onions, especially Welsh onions, have grown wild in China since prehistoric times. Early records indicate that it was in western China where people began cultivating the onion for the kitchen. Bunching onions have historically been prized for their sweet, fine flavor. They were a favorite of the Romans (what allium wasn't) and remain a favorite in kitchen gardens in Asia, Europe, and America.

Chives have also been loved for their sweet flavor. However, according to the Roman poet Marcus Martialis (circa A.D. 100), chives were also potent enough to thwart a possible kiss on the lips: "He who bears chives on his breath is safe from being kissed to death." The discovery of this verse proves to some skeptics that chives did indeed grow in Greece and Italy. They grew

*The leek has long been savored for its sweetness, and its health benefits have been touted for centuries. This illustration is from an Italian medical handbook circa 1385.*

in the wild so prolifically that ancient Greeks and Italians never bothered to cultivate them.

Onions, garlic, and their cousins found their way into kitchens and gardens long before man began to write down recipes. Whatever form and flavor they offered, their legacy remains with us today. Through research and hard work, cooks, gardeners, and health advocates now possess an array of alliums that remains a staple food and offers to some the promise of longevity. The genus *Allium* is here to stay.

# A Gallery
# of Alliums

A look at a photo of the allium clan can cause you to question its parentage. Its members are round and squat, spiky and reedy, red and yellow, papery and grassy. With more apparent differences than likenesses, it may be better to call them a tribe. Since there are more than 1,000 types of alliums, a discussion of the varieties becomes fairly complex. Climate, soil nutrients and pH balance, and other factors not only affect where and how onions behave but also how they taste and whether or not they make you cry. Because onions have been cultivated for centuries, each variety requires specific growing conditions.

While cultivating and harvesting alliums is indeed a satisfying venture, they are a real treasure in the kitchen. Some varieties, such as hardy Welsh onions, are perennials, so once their root systems become established, you can enjoy bunches of long, tender onions that can be harvested for years if the plants are properly maintained.

Onions are respected and utilized in kitchens throughout the world. Alliums show up in appetizers, main courses, vegetable casseroles, breads, condiments, and preserves. Onions and garlic provide a daily staple for many families and offer a wealth of ethnic flair. Dishes from Italy, France, the Middle East, and the Orient have come to roost on the shore of America. I've always considered this ethnic diversity to be one of the special blessings of a nation built by immigrants.

The kitchen gardener or cook gains a delicious sense of renewal as filled mason jars line the pantry or when leeks offer themselves for harvest from season to season. With so many varieties of onions and garlic available for long-term storage, a cool, dark room with good air circulation and the right amount of humidity keeps alliums and other vegetables fresh all the way to April. The bounty can last, in some cases, until the first spring crops appear.

This section will discuss alliums in six categories: bulb onions, garlic, bunching onions, leeks, shallots, and chives. Some varieties discussed here can be grown under differing conditions and in varying agricultural zones, while others are available through commercial growers and markets throughout the growing season. The following gallery offers a selection of tried-and-true, as well as slightly exotic, alliums for the garden, kitchen table, and pantry.

# YEAR-ROUND ONION AVAILABILITY

Although growers classify onions by day length, produce buyers and retailers divide them into three different categories: spring/summer fresh varieties, fresh/storage varieties, and storage varieties. The following chart shows which varieties are available in certain geographic areas at various times of year.

 Spring/Summer Fresh Varieties

 Fresh/Storage Varieties

Fall Storage Varieties

| | | Jan. | Feb. | Mar. | Apr. | May | June | July | Aug. | Sept. | Oct. | Nov. | Dec. |
|---|---|---|---|---|---|---|---|---|---|---|---|---|---|
| Arizona | | | | | | ■ | ■ | | | | | | |
| California | Imperial Valley | | | | ■ | ■ | ■ | | | | | | |
| | Coachella Valley | | | | | ■ | ■ | | | | | | |
| | Lancaster | | | | | | | | | | ▨ | ▨ | ▨ |
| | San Joaquin/ Coastal Valleys | ▨ | | | ▨ | ▨ | ▨ | ▨ | ▨ | ▨ | ▨ | ▨ | ▨ |
| Colorado | | ▨ | ▨ | | | | | | ▨ | ▨ | ▨ | ▨ | ▨ |
| Georgia | Vidalia | | | | ■ | ■ | | | | | | | |
| Hawaii | Maui | ■ | ■ | ■ | ■ | ■ | ■ | ■ | ■ | ■ | ■ | ■ | ■ |
| Idaho | | ▨ | ▨ | | | | | | ▨ | ▨ | ▨ | ▨ | ▨ |
| Indiana, Illinois, Iowa | | ▨ | ▨ | | | | | | | ▨ | ▨ | ▨ | ▨ |
| Michigan | | ▨ | ▨ | | | | | | | ▨ | ▨ | ▨ | ▨ |
| Minnesota | | ▨ | ▨ | | | | | | | ▨ | ▨ | ▨ | ▨ |
| Nevada | | ▨ | | | | | | | ▨ | ▨ | ▨ | ▨ | ▨ |
| New Mexico | South Central | | | | | | ■ | ■ | ■ | | | | |
| | Norwest | | | | | | ■ | | | | | | |
| Nebraska, S. Dakota | | ▨ | ▨ | | | | | | | ▨ | ▨ | ▨ | ▨ |
| New York | | ▨ | ▨ | ▨ | ▨ | | | | ▨ | ▨ | ▨ | ▨ | ▨ |
| North Carolina | | | | | | | ■ | ■ | | | | | |
| Ohio | | ▨ | ▨ | | | | | | | ▨ | ▨ | ▨ | ▨ |
| Oregon | Eastern | ▨ | ▨ | ▨ | ▨ | | | | | ▨ | ▨ | ▨ | ▨ |
| | North Central | ▨ | ▨ | ▨ | ▨ | | | | | ▨ | ▨ | ▨ | ▨ |
| | Western | ▨ | ▨ | ▨ | ▨ | | | | | ▨ | ▨ | ▨ | ▨ |
| Texas | Rio Grande Valley | | | ■ | ■ | ■ | | | | | | | |
| | Wintergarden | | | | ■ | ■ | ■ | | | | | | |
| | West Texas | | | | | ■ | ■ | ■ | | | | | |
| | High Plains | | | | | | | ■ | ■ | | | | |
| Utah | | ▨ | ▨ | ▨ | | | | | | ▨ | ▨ | ▨ | ▨ |
| Washington | | ▨ | ▨ | ▨ | ▨ | | | | ▨ | ▨ | ▨ | ▨ | ▨ |
| | Walla Walla | | | | | | | ■ | ■ | | | | |
| Wisconsin | | ▨ | ▨ | | | | | | | ▨ | ▨ | ▨ | ▨ |
| Canada | | ▨ | ▨ | | | | | | | ▨ | ▨ | ▨ | ▨ |
| Central/South America | Nicaragua | ■ | | | | | | | | | | | ■ |
| | Honduras | ■ | ■ | | | | | | | | | | |
| | Panama | ■ | ■ | | | | | | | | | | |
| | Chile | | | | | | | | | | | ■ | |
| | Peru | | | | | | | | | | | ■ | |
| | Uruguay | | | | | | | | | | | | |
| Mexico | Tampico | | ■ | ■ | | | | | | | | | |
| | Bajio | | | | | | | | | | ■ | ■ | |
| | Chihuahua | | | | ■ | ■ | | | | | | | |
| | Central Mexico | ■ | | | | | | | | | | ■ | ■ |

Source: Asgrow Produce Merchandising

## BULB ONIONS

With more than 1,000 varieties of onions growing today, sorting and understanding the growing conditions and physical characteristics of various hybrids can be a daunting task. However, a look at the big picture indicates that onions fall into two major categories: onions that should be used fresh or for short-term storage and onions for long-term storage.

Fresh onions include white and yellow mild, sweeter varieties that are tasty raw as well as cooked. Flattened globes such as Walla Walla and Vidalia contain more moisture and less sulphur than storage onions. These onions won't keep over the winter, but they do retain freshness and flavor for about two months under the right conditions. Storage onions include red varieties and well as some white and yellow.

### THE LONG AND THE SHORT OF IT

Northern varieties don't begin bulb development until days get to be 14 to 16 hours long, thus requiring short nights. If nights are too long, the plant produces foliage and little or no bulb. Therefore, we call these long-day onions.

Southern, or short-day, varieties require less than 12 hours of sunlight and longer nights. Sometimes, the longer nights of April and May can trigger bulbing before the plant has had the chance to develop foliage. This, too, produces small or sometimes no bulbs.

Nights, days, light intensity, and temperature all factor into bulb production, so be sure to select onions that suit your altitude and climate. If not, you may end up with a lovely green hedge and nothing to eat.

If you intend to grow your own onions, be sure to select cultivars that will develop well in your region and climate. Onion culture identifies varieties as long-, short- and intermediate-day varieties, according to the amount of daylight various strains require for bulb production. Every onion hybrid commands specific adaptations, but the standard rule divides northern and southern regions of the United States. If you live south of the imaginary line that starts between North and South Carolina and extends to San Francisco, your climate has the sun and humidity factors that make short-day types thrive. If you live in a northern area, you will want to select long-day types, which require 14 or more hours of sunlight for good bulb formation. Onions that thrive on 12 to 14 hours of sunlight are good for cultivation in intermediate-day climates, which would be states along the imaginary line.

Short-day types require less than 12 hours of light for good bulb formation and grow well in the southern states where there is more intense light and heat than in middle and northern regions of latitude. Most mail-order suppliers as well as onion culture references provide ample guidance for the allium varieties that will grow well for you. The chart on the facing page offers a view of onion-growing regions.

Onions require nutrient-rich, pH-balanced soil that is slightly sandy and loose. Well-watered and well-drained soil along with regular weeding will ensure a hearty yield. Be sure to check your soil for sulfur, nitrogen, and phosphorous content. Sulfur provides the allium with flavor, moisture control, storability, and the heat that causes tears. It is also an important ingredient for immunity from fungus, bacteria, and insects.

Stockton Red

Borretano Cipollini

On the other hand, too much nitrogen can often cause a plant to bolt and become top-heavy with foliage. When that happens, the bulbing reflex doesn't ignite, and you'll wind up with large plants with no bulbs. Phosphorous is needed to help the the bulbs mature. A lack of phosphorus as well as temperatures higher than about 60°F will get your onions off to a slow start. They need cool weather, especially during the early stages of development.

The following section offers just a few varieties of red, yellow, and white onions and information on how well they store.

### Stockton Red (Allium cepa)

The sturdy Stockton is an intermediate-day, long-term storage onion that tolerates hot weather very well and yields at 180 days in weed-free, well-watered, well-drained soil. This onion is slightly pungent with thick, somewhat coarse white flesh variegated by soft rose-colored rings. It's very digestible when eaten raw and offers hints of pepper, clove, and spice. Slice it or chop it for a succulent addition to a green salad, potato salad, table sauce, or cheese omelet. I chop it along with scallions for a spicy gazpacho. Here's a tip: Gather a bunch of Stocktons, tie a string around their long, pliant necks, and keep them handy, for you may feel compelled to use them in the kitchen on a regular basis.

### Borretano Cipollini (Allium cepa)

Although the Borretano Cipollini has long been a favorite in Italy, its arrival in the United States has been fairly recent. Both seeds and plants are available for this long-day onion that is an excellent keeper. It grows to about 1½ in. to 2 in. in diameter and has satiny skins that blush in hues of rose and bronze. This high-yield allium matures in 110 days from seed and in 75 to 80 days from transplant.

The Borretano Cipollini is a firm, somewhat squat allium, named in Italian for the button it

Red Torpedo

Rosa di Milano

resembles. It is sweet yet offers a developed allium flavor without being sharp, and it is a good candidate for storage, pickling, or marinating in balsamic vinegar. Brush a few with olive oil, lemon juice, and salt for a brief stay on the grill—no more than 10 to 12 minutes because they braise quickly. You can halve this little onion, but it is indeed meant to be eaten whole.

### Red Torpedo (Allium cepa)

This intermediate-day heirloom can be cultivated in northern regions, but it grows best in southern states. It matures faster than other reds, as it is ready for harvest about 100 days after sowing. This strain provides a consistent yield and responds to well-watered, well-drained soil.

Sometimes called the "bottle onion," this red onion is big and long (6 in. to 8 in. from tip to tip and up to 3 in. in diameter). It contains more water than other reds but will keep only for a few weeks after harvest. Make the most of

the bounty by serving this onion fresh in salads, atop enchiladas, and along with fresh corn and seafood on the grill.

### Rosa di Milano (Allium cepa)

A short-day onion that matures in about 100 days in southern states, the Rosa di Milano will store well for months in your pantry or fruit cellar. Its name comes from its beautiful color and the region in Italy that has become so well known for use of this onion in the kitchen.

This medium allium has a barrel shape that flattens out on top. The firm red flesh is mild to the taste buds and retains its sparkle whether sliced, chopped, or grated. Try it fresh over grilled poultry, fish, or a combination of peppers, corn, and summer squash. You could also serve it chopped and tossed with spaghetti squash, sautéed plum tomatoes, and fresh oregano.

Red Burgermaster

Walla Walla

### Red Burgermaster (Allium cepa)

The Red Burgermaster matures into large, round spheres in about 100 days. It is a short-day storage onion with firm red and white flesh and somewhat thick outer skin. As its name implies, it adds a fresh, mild flavor to burgers as well as to any food that yearns for a slice of crisp red onion without the tears or heat.

### Walla Walla (Allium cepa)

In northern states, the Walla Walla remains the standard long-day sweet onion. It can be sown in late summer and left to overwinter, or it can be sown in early spring and successfully transplanted. Either way, this large, sweet allium, along with the Vidalia and the Maui, is one of the first signs of spring in the kitchen. This big, somewhat flattened globe has a sweet yellowy-white flesh underneath a papery yellow skin.

The Walla Walla is mild, juicy, and can be stored for one to two months. However, it's best consumed fresh or utilized in a pot of soup or stew that can be made up and put in the freezer for the future.

I often bake and serve these onions along with baked russets and yellow sweet potatoes. However, I like them best for onion soup. The stock consists of rich chicken broth that is thick and chunky with Walla Walla and laced with sweet Marsala wine. I place a slice of dry bread and a little shredded Parmagiano-Reggiano cheese at the bottom of each soup bowl, then pour the broth over the bread and serve immediately. Some members of my family call it heaven; others say that it's as close to heaven that some of us will ever get.

*Vidalia*

*Yellow Bermuda*

## *Vidalia* (Allium cepa)

This short-day, yellow-skinned, flattened globe matures in about 160 days from seed and thrives in loose, well-watered, well-drained soil. The Vidalia's primary season extends from April through June, but certain climate conditions enable it to remain available in October and November.

The Vidalia offers crisp, sweet flesh that belies just a hint of heat. In fact, it contains probably the least amount of the sulphur that characterizes onions. It is delicious raw, sautéed, or baked into vegetable casseroles and especially onion lasagne.

## *Yellow Bermuda* (Allium cepa)

This large, juicy, sweet onion is a rose by any other name; it's actually a Spanish onion that still carries the name of a strain of allium that

became extinct some years ago. Plants mature approximately 110 days after sowing and yield big, round globes with yellow skin and pale, soft flesh tinged with a hint of yellow.

The Bermuda turns golden when cooked or sautéed, adding color as well as plenty of flavor to food. This allium is just hot enough to taste best when cooked as opposed to raw. It's a good all-purpose onion that is available year-round.

## *Yellow Globe* (Allium cepa)

The Yellow Globe grows well in just about every zone and reaches maturity 100 to 110 days after sowing. Vigorous plants yield firm, medium-to-large bulbs with yellow flesh and golden brown skin.

This long-term storage onion is creamy, full of flavor, and adds a medium-to-hot pungency to

*Yellow Globe*

*Ailsa Craig*

*Snow Baby*

food. It turns golden brown when sautéed, making it a perfect candidate for sauces and rich soup stock. Try baking slices of Yellow Globe along with garlic, basil, parsley, and butter for a simple yet satisfying addition to lunch or supper. While much of the Yellow Globe's heat disappears with cooking, it definitely adds flavor intensity to any heated dish.

## *Ailsa Craig* (Allium cepa)

This mild British cultivar has been adapted to very long days due to England's latitude. It matures in 110 days and is well liked by gardeners who enjoy raising huge, exhibition-size onions. The cool weather found in northern and eastern areas, along with a little coddling, can produce bulbs that weigh two and even three pounds.

The Ailsa is a short-term keeper with medium pungency that has become a favorite for meat pot pies and vegetable turnovers. Since this

*Sun King*

*Spanish Crystal Wax*

onion is high in water content, plan to make the most of it throughout the harvest season and into fall.

### Snow Baby (Allium cepa)

An excellent all-purpose white pearl onion with a distinct crunch, the Snow Baby matures 55 to 60 days after sowing. Start this onion in the early spring for a crop that will keep you supplied from late May to early summer. This onion grows to 1 in. to 2 in. in diameter and has a creamy white luster. You can put a few Snow Babies in the freezer to use for wintertime stew or use them for pickling or canning along with your favorite beets or cucumbers.

### Sun King (Allium cepa)

This huge Spanish hybrid matures in 112 days and often yields onions up to 5 in. in diameter. Bulbs have yellow skin and mild, juicy flesh. You would think that this cultivar wouldn't store very well, but it does. Keep a few in the pantry or fruit cellar so they last into the winter months. Sun King adds aroma and flavor to pasta, rice, and egg dishes, as well as to soups and breads.

### Spanish Crystal Wax (Allium cepa)

This prolific allium matures in 60 days with high-yielding plants that don't take up much garden space. This onion tastes best when sown in the early spring and harvested when bulbs are ½ in. to ¾ in. in diameter. The mild flavor offered by the Spanish Crystal Wax allows it to marry well with other vegetables and a variety of herbs. This and other crystal wax varieties make excellent pickling and storing onions.

### Potato Onions (Allium cepa)

The Potato Onion is an heirloom multiplier onion that gained its name because it reproduces underground like potatoes. It is also a perennial that can be planted in the early fall and wintered over or in the early spring once the ground thaws. Rather than producing seeds, this variety divides underground, producing clusters of bulbs that grow to 2 in. to 4 in. in diameter.

**Potato Onions**

This hardy allium will grow in soil or in areas where onion cultivation is typically a challenge. Once the smaller bulbs are harvested and cured, take a few to the kitchen and store them to plant later. The Potato Onion can supply your pantry nearly year-round without the task of continual replanting. Like other onions, its use in the kitchen is ubiquitous.

## GARLIC

Garlic lovers attest that of all of the members of the family *Lilliaceae*, garlic is the gem. Like so many ancient foods, it originated wild before man learned to tame and cultivate it for culinary use. Today, dedication, hard work, and downright lust for more of this allium have enabled growers to offer more strains than ever before.

### GARLIC CLASSIFICATION

| Species | *Allium sativum* | |
|---|---|---|
| Subspecies | *ophioscorodon* (hardneck) | *sativum* (softneck) |
| Varieties | Rocambole | Artichoke |
| | Continental | Silverskin |
| | Asiatic | |
| | Purple striped | |
| | Porcelain | |

Garlic varieties falls into two major subspecies: hardneck (*ophioscorodon*) and softneck (*sativum*). Within these two major categories reside dozens of marbled, glazed, striped, and porcelain strains (see the chart above on garlic classification). Some, like the Polish Hardneck, have only four large cloves clustered around a central stem. Others, such as the artichoke, hold several layers of cloves that cluster on top of each other. And depending upon moisture content, some garlics store well and some don't. The soft necks of some varieties twine easily for garlic braids and ropes, while hardnecks such as rocambole don't budge an inch.

In the kitchen, hardneck and softneck garlics offer a variety of flavors and degrees of pungency. If you are a cook who enjoys experimenting, take the opportunity to try different flavors and consistencies of garlic for eating raw or cooked. The right flavor of garlic, like a wine, will be the one that appeals to you.

Garlic grows best when planted in the fall and is ideal for cultivation in northern climates where it has the chance to winter over. Hardneck varieties bolt and form flower stalks. They typically yield large, flavor-packed cloves

*Asian Tempest*

*Carpathian*

that are easy to peel and store well for approximately eight months. Softneck, or braiding, garlic is usually easier to grow and thrives in southern climates. Many softneck varieties yield cloves that are spicier than their hardneck cousins, and they store well for up to a year, depending on climate conditions.

To grow garlic successfully, select strains that are winter-hardy in your area of the country. While this may limit the types of garlic you'll grow, you can always purchase a wide array of other bulbs for culinary experimentation. Whether you're looking for garlics for gardening or cooking, the marketplace abounds with solid, reliable everyday choices as well as varieties that may need a little extra attention or may yield a slightly exotic flavor. Both can be ordered from farms and through mail-order companies for cultivation and use in the kitchen.

### *Asian Tempest* (Allium sativum)
While Asian Tempest has been cultivated in South Korea for years, it is now available to kitchen gardeners in the United States. The

plant is vigorous with the ability to adapt to mild, wet winter climates, as well as to colder, drier regions. This garlic is graced with lush, broad green leaves and top tips that can reach 18 in. above the soil.

The genetic classification for the Asian Tempest places it in the subspecies *sativum*, as a variety of artichoke garlic. However, it behaves like hardneck garlic, producing flower stalks and yielding a single cluster of cloves around a central stalk. Happily, this anomaly is easy to grow and adds a full, tangy flavor to food. The Asian Tempest usually produces five or six medium-to-large cloves in a bulb blushing with beautiful shades of purple. It keeps well for three to six months and sometimes longer.

### *Carpathian* (Allium sativum)
The Carpathian, a hardneck member of the rocambole variety, forms large, uniform bulbs with 6 to 10 cloves that grow around a single central woody stem. Deep green leaves surround the stalk that can grow to 3 ft. to 5 ft. high with uncoiled tops. However, as is typical of hardnecks, the flower stalk, or scape, coils into tight loops as

*Metechi*

*Polish Hardneck*

the plant gains maturity. This particular characteristic encourages the nickname "serpent garlic" from gardeners fascinated by the snaky look lent by the loops leading to the umbel, or top-set capsule, and its beak, or tip.

The pale, brownish skin carries spots of rose and purple blush and is very easy to peel. It stores well, generally keeping for six months when well cultivated and cured. Possessing a strong, lingering odor, the Carpathian lends a spicy addition to soups, sauces, vegetable dishes, and meat dishes. This garlic offers endless possibilities when cooked or roasted. It's become one of my favorites for Caesar salad or steamed green beans.

### Metechi (Allium sativum)
Broad green leaves flank the stalk of the Metechi, which produces a larger bulbil capsule than most garlics. A single layer of five or six large, plump cloves surround the woody stem. A hardneck member of the purple-striped variety, this garlic has a thick white skin that blushes with intermittent batches of

purple streaks. Like other hardnecks, the Metechi is a good keeper.

This garlic offers a rich, fiery flavor when eaten raw in salads and provides a delightful appetizer when roasted with thyme and balsamic vinegar. You could also try it in a basting sauce with olive oil, Parmesan cheese, and lemon juice for grilled vegetables.

### Polish Hardneck (Allium sativum)
While a blush of purple skin covers the individual cloves, a sheath of luminous white surrounds the entire bulb. It's no wonder that this strain of garlic belongs to the porcelain group of hardnecks. The bulb usually yields just four plump, elongated globes, but it still remains comparable in size to other bulbs with more cloves. The Polish Hardneck stores well for several months and offers a rich, tangy flavor when cooked or eaten raw.

### Lorz Italian (Allium sativum)
The various strains of artichoke garlic such as the Lorz Italian produce vigorous plants with pale green leaves and stalks that do not really

*Lorz Italian*

bolt or produce flower stalks. While this garlic isn't especially photogenic, it is prolific, offering 12 to 19 cloves that cluster around a soft stem in two or three layers. Like other softneck garlics, this strain doesn't offer the rich flavor found in hardnecks, however, it's an excellent mild garlic for cooking. The Lorz Italian is good for long-term storage and is very easy to grow.

The Lorz and other types of softneck garlic such as Inchelium Red also make beautiful braids for your kitchen or as a gift for a fellow cook. These garlics dry easily and their stems become brittle. Just cover them with a moist towel for one to two days, then the stems will soften up nicely for braiding.

## BUNCHING ONIONS

Bunching onions, also called spring onions, represent smaller versions of their bulb onion cousins. However, they form a separate species because the true bunching onion forms little or no bulb. A number of bunching onions receive the bulb-onion classification *Allium cepa*,

but the true bunching onion or scallion belongs to the *Allium fistulosum* strain, which is Japanese in origin.

Like their bulb-producing relatives, bunching onions can be cultivated on either a spring or fall planting schedule. For best results, sow your onions in loose, well-drained, weed-free, pH-balanced soil that is low in sulphur. Plant them ¼ in. deep in rows 8 in. to 12 in. apart. Most varieties of scallions, hardy Welsh onions, and the more delicately flavored Japanese strains remain resistant to disease and insects when crops are rotated and the soil is regularly turned with a cultivator. Seedlings emerge 10 to 20 days after planting, and you can begin harvesting the smaller plants for kitchen use at 50 to 60 days. Depending upon the variety, mature bunching onions can reach a height of 12 in. to 14 in.

Some heartier types of bunching onions, such as the Hardy White Evergreen, will form perennial nonbulbing clumps. To maintain bunching onions and scallions as perennials, pull up the clump when harvesting, divide it, and replant as many stalks as you like. You should see a new crop the following season.

Enjoy bunching onions and scallions fresh throughout the spring and summer months. Some varieties can be dried and kept for use when colder weather reminds us that warming breezes and a new crop of alliums remain a few weeks away.

### Welsh Bunching Onions (Allium fistulosum)

This nearly bulbless perennial looks very much like large, coarse chives with long, hollow evergreen leaves. Young plants appear after 60 days and mature for harvesting at 120 days. Welsh onions should be cultivated in moist but well-

*Welsh Bunching Onions*

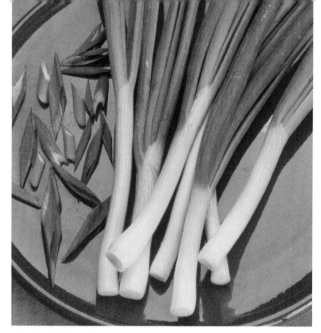

*Hardy White Evergreen*

drained soil. You can sow this allium in August, allowing it to winter over for harvest in April or May, or plant it in monthly intervals beginning in March and extending into June for a summer crop.

The young leaves of this allium can be used in stir-frys and salads or even as a substitute in recipes that call for chives. The *Allium fistulosum* is widely used in Japanese and Chinese cooking, but this onion actually came to Wales and Western Europe by way of Russia in the early 1600s, centuries after its prehistoric cousin grew wild in China.

## Hardy White Evergreen
### (Allium fistulosum)
Gardeners from the Pacific and Gulf Coast regions and a number of southern states can enjoy a healthy yield when sowing the Hardy White Evergreen from fall to early spring. Other geographic areas offer a growing season that begins in March and extends to midsummer.

This mild green scallion makes an excellent raw companion or garnish to salads, rice, or pasta. It is also a good candidate for stir-frying or quick steaming, but keep in mind that the mild flavor quickly disappears with too much heat. Enjoy this allium with a dip of olive oil blended with lemon juice and fresh chopped parsley, or serve it with other vegetables for a first course of aïoli or *bagna cauda* and crusty, fresh bread.

## Koba Japanese Scallions
### (Allium fistulosum)
While the Koba thrives in tropical climates, it also produces well in hot, slightly drier areas as long as it is cultivated in loose, weed-free soil that receives regular mists of water. This plant yields delicate, hollow, pale green leaves atop a slender, bulbless base. Unlike heartier scallion varieties, this allium looks very much like a chive while tasting like an extremely mild scallion. Use the Koba raw, dried, or frozen as a flavorful addition to soups, breads, grains, pasta, or Asian stir-frys.

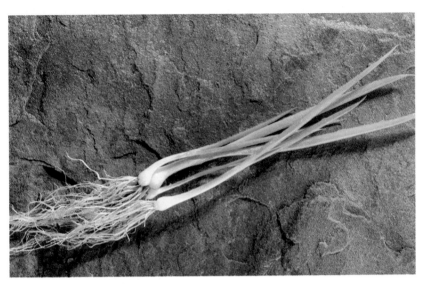

*Koba Japanese Scallions*

*Egyptian Bunching Onions*

## *Egyptian Bunching Onions*
## (Allium cepa)

Also known as the tree or catawissa onion, the Egyptian should be sown in the fall for a spring crop. It is among the heartiest of the allium perennials, while bearing physical characteristics and behavior that set it apart from other strains. The Egyptian produces a head of up to 16 small onions instead of flowers, but there are cases where a second umbel grows out of the first and *does* produce flowers.

Although this onion is genetically classified as bulbing, its base is rounded rather than swollen. You can divide the plant bulbs for future crops or simply allow this onion to "walk" its way across the garden. Since this allium is top set, the slender shoots cannot remain erect under the weight of the bulbils. The plant bends to the ground, the tops take root, and another generation of Egyptian onions takes off. You can use the entire plant for any recipe that requires fresh raw onions, or enjoy them grilled with salmon, potatoes, and herbs.

## LEEKS

The prospect of growing leeks may seem a bit daunting, but once you try a few in your garden, you'll be pleasantly surprised. They are very easy to grow and are a money saver for the cook who enjoys using them in the kitchen. These alliums can be very expensive at the supermarket, so the opportunity to harvest them all year long could prove to be well worth the investment of your time and energy.

The trick to growing leeks with long, white stems (the part used in cooking) is a technique called hilling, or blanching. Throughout the growing season, hill the soil around the base of the plants, and keep the plants trimmed to 3 in. to 4 in. above the lowest leaf. Hilling the soil forces the leek to reach toward the sun, which forces growth in the lower stem, or white shank. Without this process, you may produce quite a large green upper stem and very little white.

Once leeks mature, they stop gaining volume and can literally stay in the ground through snow and freezing weather. The leaves can burn and turn brown, but the plant will stay alive. You can plant these offbeat alliums in May for a crop that extends into November, or you can plant them in the early fall for leeks that will take you through the winter and into spring. You can wait to harvest leeks until they fully mature, but young leeks are delicious and considered to be a delicacy.

Leeks come in different sizes and shades of green to blue-green. Each strain also offers a subtle difference in flavor, so plant more than one variety. You'll enjoy the opportunity to blend the variations with other mild onions, herbs, and vegetables. Leeks add a fresh, mellow sweetness to soups, fennel, pot pies, and just about any recipe that calls for a mild onion.

*Bleu de Solaise*

### *Bleu de Solaise* (Allium ampheloprasm)

This French heirloom may require a little patience as it seems to get off to a slow start, but plenty of fertile soil, mulching, and a weed-free environment will ensure an allium that grows well over several weeks. The white edible portion of this leek should not be harvested until it reaches 1 in. in diameter. The Bleu de Solaise (also known as the purple St. Victor leek) carries stunning royal purple leaves. While this allium can be planted in either the early spring or fall, its leaves gain color and the bulb intensifies with flavor once dusted by frost. Just remember that overwintered leeks should be harvested in the early spring before they produce a seed stalk. At that stage of growth, the white shank becomes tough, fibrous, and inedible.

### *Albinstar* (Allium ampheloprasm)

The Albinstar is a Dutch variety that has been specifically developed to produce succulent baby leeks. Maturing about 110 days after planting, this variety offers a shank that is usually no wider than ½ in. to ⅝ in. in diameter. The flesh is very tender and is a good candidate for grilling or stovetop roasting. However, the Albinstar also grows into a tall, hardy plant with an equally delicious shaft with a more mature flavor. Both options provide a bounty of flavor.

### *Falltime* (Allium ampheloprasm)

The Falltime doesn't winter over well, so plant it in the early spring for a fall harvest. This cultivar is known to grow as much as 3 ft. long while retaining tenderness and excellent flavor. It matures in 80 to 90 days, offering an early yield of sweet, mild-flavored leeks.

### *Scotland* (Allium ampheloprasm)

This hardy, high-yielding heirloom variety matures in 85 to 90 days and winters over very well. The white shank offers a crisp yet tender flesh with a slightly more vibrant onion flavor than other leeks. It makes an excellent potato-leek soup, as well as a bread stuffing with sage for poultry.

*Albinstar*

*Falltime*

*Scotland*

## *Elephant Garlic*
## (Allium ampheloprasm)

Although this bulb bears a creamy, mild, and delicious garlic flavor, it is, by species, a strain of leek. However, if you want the taste of garlic without the strong, lingering side effects, this variety of leek is a good choice. Plant it in the fall or early spring because it requires cool weather for early stages of development, then harvest and cure it when the tops begin to fall.

Elephant garlic is delicious raw in salads and vinaigrette dressing and when roasted, sautéed, or steamed with vegetables. It keeps well and will bless your spaghetti sauce with flavor long after autumn graces the landscape with splashes of gold, russet, and orange.

## SHALLOTS

Shallots are related to onions, but they are milder in flavor. They are just as easy to grow, but I have always made note of the difference in price. Shallots tend to be quite costly at the supermarket, regardless of the season. Once you've harvested a few, you'll wonder why.

*Elephant Garlic*

*Atlantic*

*French Gray*

*Success*

You can enjoy fresh shallots nearly year-round, just by planting a few bulbs in the early spring. Insert the bulb in the soil, root side down, with the tip of the shallot slightly uncovered. Since this allium belongs to the *aggregatum*, or multi-plier, group, one bulb will produce a whole cluster. Like other members of the *aggregatum* group, shallots are also perennial bulbs. If you harvest and store shallots like onions and then reinvest some in the earth, you'll not be shocked by prices at the supermarket again.

Shallots combine well with herbs for vinaigrette dressing, but they are best when roasted, sautéed, or steamed, as the full benefit of their special flavor can only be released by heat.

### *Atlantic* (Allium cepa)

The Atlantic Dutch shallot is large, plump, and round with a vibrant golden-tan skin. The Atlantic stores well, so you can keep a few on hand all winter long. Full of flavor yet very mild, this shallot harmonizes well with sautéed balsamic leeks, scallions, and baby carrots.

### *Success* (Allium cepa)

Success offers a unique blend of garlic and onion flavors. The firm, tender bulb is graced with a glowing auburn shell, making this allium beautiful as well as tasty. Try it in soups, with sautéed mushrooms, or sauté it and serve with grilled sole or atop a thick slice of fresh, hot, buttered bread.

Frog's Leg

Chinese Garlic Chives

Mauve Chives

## *French Gray* (Allium cepa)

This long, large shallot is probably the most prized variety among those who prepare French cuisine. The dull, gray skin completely masks the treasure inside. When roasted, this flesh transforms into a creamy, redolent appetizer or a flavorful addition to any number of soups, side dishes, and main courses. Try roasting it with a little olive oil, thyme, rosemary, salt, pepper, and balsamic vinegar. The consistency and flavor are special indeed.

## *Frog's Leg* (Allium cepa)

A small, slender yet firm shallot, the Frog's Leg does resemble the physical characteristics of a frog's leg, but be assured that the bulb enclosed by the glowing auburn outer skin tastes like nothing amphibious. This shallot makes an excellent flavor addition to soups, either roasted or raw. The flavor combines well with winter squash, apples, pasta, and risotto.

## CHIVES

Although some say that sweet onions herald the new growing season, I find that chives turn green as soon as the snow melts. Whether they are white or mauve, chives add grace to the garden and offer a multitude of opportunities in the kitchen. These hardy perennials respond well to regular snipping. Harvested chives can be finely snipped and frozen or dried for future use. Their delicate flavor harmonizes with russets, new potatoes, herbs, and butter. You can use chives in a salad dressing or in a marinade for your favorite grilled salmon or chicken.

## *Chinese Garlic Chives* (Allium tuberosum)

This perennial is easy to grow and offers a slightly more intense flavor than the mauve chive. The garlic chive requires neutral, well-watered, well-drained soil, as well as separating and transplanting from season to season to prevent the broad, flat stalks from growing into dense, unattractive clumps. In the kitchen, combine garlic chives, lemon verbena, white pepper, and butter to taste, then refrigerate for two to three days, and use atop steaks and chicken for the grill.

## *Mauve Chives* (Allium schoenprasm)

The mauve chive looks much like a young scallion: round, hollow, and pale green. Yet this chive is more tender and far more delicate in flavor. This mild, sweet allium needs well-watered, well-drained soil and responds well to snipping and thinning.

# Harvesting and Storing

If onions and their cousins are easy to grow, then the process that preserves their flavor and freshness is even simpler. It begins in the garden, as the time for harvesting and storing draws near.

When managing your kitchen garden or selecting produce from a local vendor, remember that firm, bright produce promises good nutrition and flavor. This rule holds true for onions, which have a distinct advantage over some vegetables because their chemical compounds ensure vitamin and flavor retention long after they've been picked. In addition, onions don't lose a percentage of their nutritional value when cooked, as many vegetables, such as peppers, do.

## BULB ONIONS

Bulb onions should be harvested once their tops turn brown and bend toward the ground. Dig or pull them out of the ground to dry once you can anticipate about two weeks without rain. Leave them on the ground for a day or two, then transfer them to large screens or baskets and let them cure in a shady place for another 10 to 14 days. Most of the dirt will fall off, or can be easily rubbed off, before placing the bulbs on screens or in baskets. When the

*Onions are ready for harvesting once their tops begin to fall. Dig or pull them out of the ground, and allow them to rest on the dirt, uncovered, for a couple of days before transferring them to screens for curing.*

*Onions are not only one of the oldest foods but also can be stored longer than most. Whether red, white, or yellow, storage varieties keep well under proper conditions for three months.*

mesh bags or to a well-ventilated basket or box and place them in a cool, dark place. Never mound or stack onions because they won't ventilate and will begin to rot.

The two-step process of curing then storing prolongs the length of time that your onions will last and retain their flavor. A little patience with the curing allows many varieties to last until April.

Unlike bunching onions, the green tops and leaves of other fresh and storage types are not edible. The foliage is coarse and fibrous with a strong, somewhat bitter flavor, making it a better candidate for flavoring soup stock. The white bulb, however, should be crisp and glistening with moisture and flavor.

## GARLIC
Like bulb onions and shallots, garlic is ready for harvesting once the tops have fallen. Garlic bulbs need to be somewhat dry when they're removed from the garden, so gradually decrease their water for three to four days before harvesting. When harvesting, dig, rather than pull, the bulbs from dry soil. This is especially important for slightly fragile softneck varieties. If you begin by pulling, you may end up with damaged plants or, more than likely, a stem without a bulb.

Replication of soil, humidity, and light conditions is crucial when harvesting your garlic, so plan ahead to create a storage environment that is devoid of direct sun and as close as possible to the temperature and humidity of your garden. Sudden changes in temperature can cause alliums' cell walls to expand and contract rapidly. This affects the composition of the individual cloves and can affect storability.

*Softneck garlic can add a bit of art to your kitchen when braided. The garlic should be braided while the shaft and leaves are still supple; if necessary, cover with a moist kitchen towel for a couple of days to regain pliability.*

skins have turned opaque and dry, the onions are ready for storage or immediate use.

You may want to take onions with thicker necks directly to the kitchen, for they don't tend to store very well. Transfer the others to

Once you've dug up the plants, spread them on screens in a shady spot or shed for a few days or until the dirt around the bulb can be rubbed away. Soils in some zones can be very tight and dense, making it difficult to remove the dirt. The temptation is to wash off the bulb, but resist doing this because moisture causes molds that lead to rot. It's best to alter soil conditions at the outset with plenty of humus and mulching.

Placing garlic, shallots, and bulb onions on screens helps the drying process by allowing air to circulate freely around the bulbs. If you wish to make your own screen setup, use 2x4s to build a box frame no larger than 48 in. square, then nail a sturdy metal screen to one side. Position the box so that the screen side is off the surface or ground. If you plan to harvest and cure a sizable crop, you may want to build two or three screens or devise a larger setup. The frames do tend to get heavy, and each screen can hold a limited quantity before sagging.

Once the garlic has cured, remove the dried foliage from the bulbs, then place the bulbs in a basket or mesh bag for storage. Softneck garlics can be braided and hung in a cool spot away from direct sun in your pantry or kitchen.

*While some varieties of bunching onions do produce a slight bulb, this species is known for its straight white shank. Regardless of flavor and heat, bunching onions add form and aesthetic appeal to any garden.*

With a few simple precautions, you can enjoy garlic as well as shallots for several months.

## BUNCHING ONIONS

When it's time for harvesting, bunching onions such as scallions can be pulled or dug up from the ground, cleaned thoroughly, and brought to the kitchen table. These alliums should have erect green tops and leaves that show plenty of color. The flesh should be firm and devoid of scrapes or brown spots. Bunching onions store well in the refrigerator for only a few days.

## LEEKS

Leeks are planted in the early spring or, depending on variety, in the early fall before the first frost. They can be harvested any time through the late fall and early winter and, in the case of those varieties that can withstand the cold, whenever the ground is not frozen. If you enjoy baby leeks, simply harvest them at an earlier stage of development.

Leeks can be harvested and stored like many root vegetables. Leave their tops attached to the white shank and lay these alliums on their sides in slightly damp sand in a cold room or

*Rows of hardneck garlic gain the attributes of a small forest as summer yields to fall. Straight, firm trunks bear dark green leaves that stretch toward the sky.*

*Cure onions and garlic on screens in a shady, well-ventilated spot. They need plenty of good air circulation and protection from rain and sunburn.*

fruit cellar. Or, as allium pro Louis Van Deven suggests, *do* trim the tops and keep a bunch of leeks in the vegetable drawer of your refrigerator. In fact, leeks retain so much body and flavor this way that you may find yourself shopping for a second refrigerator—leeks take up a lot of room!

With the exception of baby varieties, leeks' foliage is tough and quite inedible. You may want to trim the leaves of larger leeks back a bit before storing in the refrigerator. Try reserving 3 in. to 4 in. of the green stem for flavoring your next pot of soup.

## SHALLOTS

Shallots should also be harvested once the tops have fallen. As shallots mature, you should move the soil away from the base of the stalk so that the bulb gets more exposure to the sun. When you can plan on a few continuous days of sun, ease bulbs that are plump, firm, and free of green burn spots and bruises out of the ground. Allow them to dry on the ground before moving them onto a screen or to any other well-ventilated spot.

When curing, try not to crowd bulbs too closely together so that they get good air ventilation. Allowing the skins to dry and the necks to shrivel prevents the formation of damaging molds that cause bulb rot. After shallots have cured, which should take 10 to 14 days, they can then be stored in your refrigerator or in a cool room that supplies ideal storage conditions, namely 32°F and about 60% humidity. Too much humidity will cause your bulbs to sprout and too little will create dry, tasteless, and tough shallots.

*While leeks and onions are harvested at different stages of growth, the requirements for quality remain the same. Look for firm, bright, slightly translucent flesh that is free from scratches, bruises, and dents.*

## CHIVES

Chives can be harvested at any time throughout the growing season. The shafts should be erect, firm, and bright green. Snip them with scissors frequently to encourage more growth. These tender, mild alliums can be transferred to the kitchen for immediate use.

## LONG-TERM ALLIUM STORAGE

It's hard to know all of the reasons behind the quest for the bulb onion, but its universal appeal is historical and legendary. Its health benefits and its suitability for cultivation prob-

*Some varieties of onions, garlic, shallots, and leeks are perfect candidates for canning and pickling. A small investment in canning gear, a few good recipes, and adherence to basic procedures yield a bounty of pantry treasures long into the colder months.*

ably helped mankind not only survive several plagues but also feed families when other crops failed. Bulb onions are survivors and many are keepers. Among the methods used to store onions for long amounts of time include canning, pickling, and dehydrating.

### Canning and pickling
Most alliums aren't good candidates for canning, but a few varieties of small, white storage onions, such as pearl onions, are delicious when pickled and processed in a boiling-water bath.

Some varieties of storage onions can be blended for cooked salsas, sauces, and condiments. When canning or pickling, always select alliums that are fresh, firm, and free of nicks and spots. Damaged or bruised flesh can frequently cause spoilage.

Since vinegar is the key ingredient for pickling, look for one that contains 5% to 6% acidity. By doing this, your produce will retain flavor and keep well in the pantry for months.

Work with any pickling recipe that seems attractive, remembering that the salt and vinegar contents are essential to a successful batch of pickled onions, which should be crisp and flavorful weeks after processing.

Canning and pickling require some advance planning, so take the time to gather the necessary containers and utensils: pint or half-pint jars, a boiling-water-bath canner, lids, rims, a funnel, clamps, racks, hot pads, and long-handled dippers and spoons.

State extension offices as well as a number of canning guides and books offer step-by-step information about how to can fresh produce based on your geographical region and altitude. You may want to do a little reading up before beginning the adventure. Most guides offer a discussion along with photos and helpful illustrations that will enable you to see the entire process from beginning to end.

Here are some guidelines for canning success regardless of where you live.

- Make sure all utensils and jars are sterile and hot.

- Inspect jar rims and lids for possible cracks. Any inconsistency can impair the effectiveness of the seal.

- Wipe the rims of the jars with a clean, damp, lint-free cloth to remove any stray particles of dust or food. Flecks of material on the rim will more than likely prevent the formation of a vacuum that is crucial for storability.

- When using a boiling-water bath, fill the canner at least one-third of the way with water and bring it to a boil. Place the jars in the bath, then add enough water to immerse them. Preferably, the jars should reside about ½ in. below the surface of the water.

- Bring the bath back to a boil before clocking the processing time.

- Once your processing time is complete, gently lift the jars from the bath and place them in a quiet, draft-free spot in the kitchen. The lids should pop and the jars should be completely cooled before you transfer them to the pantry.

- Always look for spoilage in canned foods. If you see a bulge in the lid, open the jar. If the food has a sour taste or odor, spoilage has occurred and, in some cases, poisonous botulism is developing.

This information along with the canning guidelines for your area should ensure treasures from the pantry months after the harvest moon has waned.

### Dehydrating

Food dehydrators offer the best results when drying onions, some garlics, and chives. These machines provide the heat and air circulation to effectively dehydrate the fibrous allium. To use this method, wash and chop your onions into small pieces about ½ in. to 1 in. long, then follow the instructions that have been provided with the unit you've purchased. Most onions will dry after 12 to 24 hours in the dehydrator, looking light and papery when done. In most cases, 1¼ cups of raw onions will yield 1 cup of dried.

Dried onions need to cook for 20 to 30 minutes when added to your recipes. They will not only regain volume but will also offer a wonderful, toasty, steeped flavor to food.

*Garlic, as well as a variety of onions, can be braided and hung in the kitchen or pantry for future use. Here a cluster of blushing Torpedo onions glow in the afternoon sun.*

I was surrounded by alliums in the kitchen last summer. Braids of garlic and shallots were strung along the wall beside the refrigerator. A gathering basket brimming with iridescent cipollini graced the counter. The kitchen table held mounds of yellow, white, and red onions. Some were fat, round bulbs that nestled under long Torpedo or bottle onions. Others were round and squat and crowned with green, lanky scallions, leeks, and chives. The arrangement of this mosaic continually changed form, as spring led to summer, then July closed its doors, allowing August to announce the height of the harvest.

As alliums made their way into my kitchen and onward to more tasteful pursuits, they became my teachers. They reminded me of the importance of a light touch, that a bruise can foster spoilage, and that certain aromas can linger interminably in curtains. They even made me cry. But with all of that, I gained a heightened appreciation when preserving the freshness and flavor of intriguing varieties of shallots, onions,

garlic, and leeks. Alliums add an arresting volume and flavor to herbs, vegetables, grains, and each other. Their use in the kitchen is ancient and ubiquitous. This section will discuss cleaning and handling alliums, cooking techniques, and flavor combinations.

## HANDLING TECHNIQUES

Whether you are working with garlic, leeks, onions, or shallots, it's a good idea to follow a few basic guidelines, some of which will reduce odors and tears.

First, always use a sharp knife. By doing this, you'll cut through hotter alliums quickly and bruise the flesh a little less.

Next, always remember to cut onions quickly and only as you need them. You may get the urge to do a little preparation work in advance, but once raw onion pieces are exposed to the air they take on different flavors and even odors. When cooking, you should get the

You can avoid at least a few tears by quartering and chilling onions for about an hour before final use. Holding them under the coldest water from your faucet also dilutes the fumes.

onions into the pot as fast as possible. If you are slicing onions for raw consumption, they can sit in a bowl of ice water until you are ready to serve.

## Reducing odors

Preparing onions, garlic, and their cousins for recipes involves a certain amount of care and caution—particularly when you're working with hotter storage onions and spicier varieties of garlic. The chemical compounds in each can be absorbed into the surface of your skin and linger for days. To remove the strong odor of onions and garlic, rinse your hands under cold water, then rub them with about 1 tablespoon of salt, and rinse again. You can also rub a cut lemon over your hands after the second rinse for a freshened scent, and rinse a third time.

The allium that scents your hands will also scent your breath. Eating an apple or rinsing your mouth with equal parts of lemon juice and water will sweeten your breath. Since abstinence isn't an option among onion and garlic lovers, you may consider sharing your food with friends or spending a few days in solitude.

## Reducing tears

Spicy storage onions contain a higher sulfur content than other varieties. When the sulfur reaches your eyes, it starts to dehydrate, thus forming sulfuric acid. This causes the sting and tears that cooks have come to reckon with. To cut down the crying, try refrigerating onions in an airtight container for at least eight hours in advance of peeling and cutting. However, if you need to act more spontaneously, you may just have to grin and bear it.

Rinsing washes away some of the harsher compounds, so try cutting onions under running water to dilute the sulfur compounds that collect at the root end. When you do cut into an onion, make sure you save the root end for last. You won't be releasing the sulfur as quickly, which may save your eyes a bit.

## ALLIUM PREPARATION

Onions, like other varieties of produce, reward us with a cornucopia of freshness and flavor when properly handled. The following tips can help reduce prep time while enhancing the blessings of the bounty.

## Bulb onions

To prepare bulb onions, slice the bulb horizontally at the stem, then use a sharp knife to peel the skin by pulling it toward the root end. If you want to slice the onion, cut it horizontally, starting at the peeled stem and working back toward the root end. When you want to dice or chop an onion, cut it in vertical halves or thirds before working toward the root end. If you are using a food processor, cut the stem and root end off the onion, slice it in half, then process using your desired blade. If you're grating by hand, cut off the stem but leave the root end intact.

## Boiling onions, cipollini, and pearls

Smaller onions, particularly firmer storage types, peel very easily when dropped into boiling water for about 1 minute, then plunged into cold water for a quick chill and drained. These onions can be processed whole or in halves. When the onions are cool enough to handle, use a sharp knife to cut off the ends and remove the skin.

## Scallions

Scallions should be thoroughly rinsed to remove any loose dirt captured in the roots and leaves. Begin processing scallions by cutting off the rough, tougher green parts and discarding them. Next, cut the scallion in half lengthwise, then place the flat, or cut, side of each half onto your work surface. From here, you can start at the bulb end to make small horizontal cuts for varying lengths of scallion. The use of a very sharp knife is especially helpful when you get to the foliage.

It's best to slice an onion beginning at the stem end and working toward the root, where the sulfur collects. Two vertical halves can also be a little easier to handle when you are preparing to slice or dice onions into smaller pieces.

You'll want to chop or dice onions quickly to avoid the fumes that cause tears. Cut or chop the onions on a firm surface using a very sharp knife or cleaver.

To prep your leeks for cooking, cut off the root end and the darker green leaves. They are fibrous and too chewy to be palatable, but you may want to clean and store them in the refrigerator for your next pot of soup stock.

The leek's white shank needs to be thoroughly rinsed to remove any grit and sand imbedded between the layers. Cutting the shank in half vertically makes for easy handling.

Using a sharp knife or cleaver, slice the leek into thin vertical strips...

...or dice it for soups, stews, and casseroles.

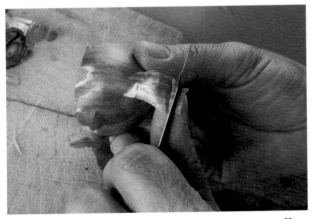

*Peel a shallot as you would an onion by cutting off the stem and peeling the outer skin to the root end.*

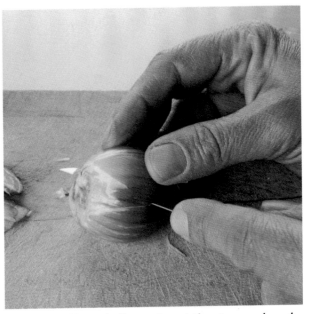

*Cut the shallot in half, starting at the stem and working toward the root end.*

## Leeks

When leeks are brought in from the garden, their crevices usually contain little mounds of sandy dirt. While some dirt will be visible, much of it hides in between the layers of greenery that are closest to the shank. This allium needs to be thoroughly cleaned or you'll find unwanted sand in your soup or on your tongue. To prepare a leek, cut off the roots and the tough green leaves where they meet the shank. Using a very sharp knife, cut the leek in half lengthwise, gently fan it open, and rinse it under cold tap water until all the sandy grit has been removed. You may want to pat it dry or let it drain before slicing or dicing for your recipe.

## Shallots

Peeling shallots, particularly the large French Gray, requires a sharp knife. The skin on the gray shallot is thick and tough, so you will want to cut off both ends and remove all of the skin before slicing. Other varieties of shallots are easier to peel, which you can do by simply cutting off the stem and peeling the skin toward the root end. Cut shallots in half lengthwise, then slice or dice as you would an onion.

*A mezzaluna chops shallots, as well as smaller onions, garlic, and scallions, with ease.*

*Fresh chives should be snipped with scissors.*

## Chives

This delicate allium requires no knife at all. Use scissors to snip your chives into small pieces; they're less likely to bruise this way.

## COOKING TECHNIQUES

According to respected food historian Waverly Root, some people believe that the onion's true origin is indeed diabolical. That's probably because ancient Turkish legend says that when Satan was cast from heaven, sulfur came forth from his feet once he landed. Garlic sprouted where he first placed his left foot and onions sprouted under the influence of his right.

To this day, sulfur collects at the root ends of onions with a strength that pervades the air and causes a few tears once this allium is cut. The antidote to the pain, of course, lies in cooking and baking, for heat dissipates much of the chemical and transforms the "diabolic" allium into a palatable and harmless food. Even if you prefer your onions raw, the following methods offer some tips for retaining plenty of flavor and texture.

## Stuffing onions

Medium onions as well as smaller boiling onions are delicious when stuffed and baked. You simply need to remove a bit of the center in preparation for your particular recipe. Begin by slicing and processing medium onions the same way you process smaller boiling types.

Using a sharp knife, make a crosscut at the stem end of an onion. Then, with the end of a paring knife, gently pull out the very center of the bulb. If you are prepping a slightly larger onion and want to create a larger bowl, remove the center and the next layer of the onion as well. The onion, whether little or large, now awaits its stuffing. (See the recipe for Onions Vodka on p. 58.)

## Braising onions

Braised yellow and white onions are used whenever a recipe calls for rich, brown color. They can be cooked a few hours or even a day in advance, then reheated for final assembly.

For 4 to 5 cups of sliced onions, heat 2 tablespoons of olive oil and 1½ tablespoons of butter in a large skillet. Add the onions and sauté for 10 to 15 minutes, stirring constantly to keep them covered with the oil and butter. Next, add ½ cup of dry red wine, salt and white pepper to taste, and a bay leaf. Cover and cook over medium heat for 35 to 45 minutes. When

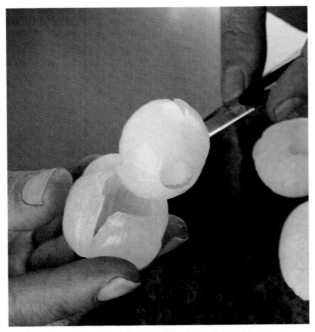

To prepare an onion for stuffing, it's best to remove the center in layers in order to cause less strain on the outer shell, which is fairly delicate and easy to tear.

Gently remove the very center of the onion with the tip of a sharp knife.

Use a small spoon to fill the onion bowls with the filling of your choice.

Boiling onions make excellent bite-size appetizers. These are filled with sour cream and caviar (see the recipe on p. 58).

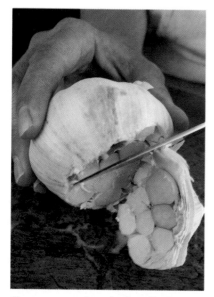

*To prepare a head of garlic for roasting, use a sharp knife to slice off the stem end. Remove any loose outer skin with your fingers.*

*A head of garlic simply needs herbs, balsamic vinegar, and a little time in the oven. The reward for your efforts will be a creamy, flavorful appetizer or side dish that's well worth the wait.*

done, the onions should be tender and the liquid should be evaporated. Remove the bay leaf and serve or add the onions to your recipe. One pound of onions will serve three or four people as a side dish.

### Roasting garlic

Roasted garlic is delicious as an appetizer and adds dimension to butters, soups, rice, and main dishes. Once you get accustomed to roasting garlic, you'll probably find yourself experimenting with a number of recipes. Roasted garlic celebrates a mild, nutty flavor that easily combines with others. The flavor is subtle yet rich and known by some to be slightly addictive.

To roast three or four bulbs of garlic, preheat the oven to 325°F. After cutting off the root ends, place the garlic in a shallow baking dish or terra-cotta baker. Brush the garlic heads with a little olive oil and bake for 35 to 45 minutes, then remove from the oven and set aside until cool enough to handle. The garlic should be tender and easily squeezed out of the skin of each clove. You may want to test the garlic by pricking it with a paring knife before removing it from the oven. If the garlic remains a bit resistant, allow it to bake a little longer.

You can follow the same principle for roasting shallots. However, preheat the oven to 350°F and allow the shallots to bake for 25 to 30 minutes.

## FLAVOR COMBINATIONS

Onions add flavor to any recipe and offer a multitude of possibilities when combined with other foods. Mixing onions and their cousins—scallions, leeks, shallots, and garlic—provides a delightful trio of heat, sweetness, and volume. You can sauté them together and serve as a side dish, or try slicing and layering various alliums, placing them in a lightly oiled ovenproof dish, and baking until tender.

Some onions hold their body under heat better than others:

- Red onions are best when eaten raw or quickly grilled. They lose their color and become watery when cooked.

- Various mild as well as spicy storage onions retain their body and even improve their flavor when cooked. Milder Walla Walla, Vidalia, and Maui types make succulent participants in main courses, soups, and casseroles. Yellow onions turn to a deeper, golden brown when cooked or sautéed. Varieties such as Spanish onions and Yellow Globes add a rich, steeped flavor and color to soups, sauces, and gravies.

Most varieties of white storage onions hold up under heat and actually become a little sweeter during cooking. Heat causes the sugar

> ### GARLIC AND ONION EQUIVALENTS
>
> 1 medium clove garlic = ⅛ teaspoon, minced
>
> 1 pound of sliced onions = 3½ to 4 cups
>
> 1 medium onion = 2½ to 3 ounces, or ½ to ⅝ cup, chopped

volume of onions to expand, thus many onions lose the hot bite they carried when they were removed from the earth.

- Smaller onions such as cipollini, boiling onions, and baby pearls remain quite sturdy when simmered or pickled. Try mixing the different types together in one batch of pickled fare. You'll find a few surprises that will send you back to the jar for more.

- The noble leek combines regal flavor with good storability. Perhaps that's why this turgid allium bends and swoons within the confines of the saucepan or soup pot yet doesn't expire. If anything, the leek gains flavor while keeping its posture when things heat up. That could be part of the reason for French folk crowning it the queen of the kitchen.

- Shallots and garlic have been blessed with sturdy outer skins that do double duty when these alliums meet heat. Since the flesh of garlic and shallots cook to soft, creamy morsels, the skins keep the bulbs intact.

# Recipes

# Appetizers

*Artichoke with Garlic-Chive Sauce and Spring Greens (recipe on page 56)*

# ARTICHOKE WITH GARLIC-CHIVE SAUCE AND SPRING GREENS

6 large shrimp
Garlic-Chive Sauce, 1 recipe
1 large fresh artichoke
3 tablespoons lemon juice
2 cups mixed baby spring
    greens

**Garlic-Chive Sauce**
2 tablespoons lemon juice
¼ cup extra-virgin olive oil
1 tablespoon lemon zest
¼ teaspoon ground red
    pepper
4 cloves garlic, minced
1 teaspoon dehydrated onion
    flakes
2 tablespoons fresh lemon
    thyme leaves
3 tablespoons chopped fresh
    chives
1 teaspoon grated Parmesan
    cheese
½ teaspoon salt

*While artichokes can be enjoyed just about any time of year, they offer extra pleasure during springtime when served with young garlic, fresh chives, and baby mixed greens. This recipe can be doubled and made a day ahead, making it easy to host a large number of guests. While this artichoke and shrimp dish can be shared as an appetizer, this combination also offers a light yet satisfying lunch when served with fresh bread and orange slices. (Photo on page 54.)*

In a small saucepan, bring about 1½ cups water to a boil, then reduce the heat. Add the shrimp and simmer 7-10 minutes, or until the shrimp are pink. Drain the shrimp and set aside until cool enough to handle. Peel the shrimp, remove the veins, and rinse under cool water. Transfer to a small bowl, and drizzle each shrimp with 1 tablespoon of the Garlic-Chive Sauce. Cover with plastic wrap, and refrigerate until ready to use.

Cut the stem from the artichoke and trim the pointed ends until the leaves are 1 inch to 1¼ inches long. Place the artichoke in a small saucepan with about 1½ cups water and the lemon juice. Cover and simmer 20-30 minutes, or until the leaves move easily when pried with a fork. Remove the artichoke from the saucepan, open the middle, then remove the choke with a teaspoon or fork and discard. Place the artichoke on a small plate and refrigerate until ready to use.

Arrange the greens on a plate, place the artichoke on the greens, then place the shrimp in the crevices between the artichoke leaves. In a blender, whir the Garlic-Chive Sauce 10 seconds, then pour over the greens or pour into a small dipping bowl or pitcher to pass for individual servings. Serve immediately.

*Serves 4*

**Garlic-Chive Sauce**

In a blender, mix the lemon juice and oil to form a creamy sauce. Add the lemon zest, red pepper, garlic, onion flakes, lemon thyme, chives, cheese, and salt, and blend 2-3 minutes.

*Yields ½ cup*

# GREEK *TARAMA* CAVIAR

4 ounces *tarama*

1 small Vidalia onion, finely chopped

1 stalk green garlic, minced

2 egg yolks

8 slices stale white bread, crust removed and torn into small pieces

¾ cup extra-virgin olive oil

½ cup lemon juice

1 teaspoon lemon zest

4 slices pita bread, cut into wedges

1 cucumber, peeled and cut into ¼-inch-thick slices

1 lemon, cut into wedges, garnish

*T*he Greek islands have been a source of enlightenment, history, and cultural enrichment for centuries. Along with music and a passion for living, the people and their kitchens offer simple yet exotic combinations of flavors. The Greeks have long understood how to make use of the fruits of the earth as well as the sea. The main ingredient for this appetizer is *tarama, or carp roe, which can be found in grocery stores that stock ethnic ingredients. Since tarama is the color of pale coral, this dip offers attractive color along with excellent flavor.*

In a blender or food processor, blend the *tarama,* onions, garlic, and egg yolks into a smooth paste. Add the white bread and blend until smooth. With the motor running, gradually drizzle in the oil, lemon juice, and lemon zest until all of the liquid has been absorbed and the ingredients are well combined.

Refrigerate at least 4 hours to allow the dip to thicken. Serve with the pita bread and cucumbers. Garnish with lemon.

*Yields 2⅔ cups; serves 6-8*

*Note: Tarama can be found in most Greek and Middle Eastern food stores. It is also available from mail-order sources.*

# ONIONS VODKA

3 eggs
8 small boiling onions, 1 inch in
    diameter
1 cup vodka
juice of 1 lemon
8 teaspoons sour cream
8 teaspoons black caviar
8 lemon wedges, garnish

*A medley of translucent white onions, black caviar, and yellow lemon wedges provides a colorful and dramatic addition to any table. All of the ingredients can be prepared in advance and assembled just before serving. A last-minute squeeze of lemon on each onion heightens the blend of flavors, and you can add melba toast or crackers to serve with the chopped egg. Vodka onions should be eaten with your fingers, but if you like larger fare, use onions that can be served on individual plates along with a fork and knife.*

In a 1-quart saucepan, cover the eggs with water, bring to a slow boil, and simmer 15 minutes. Remove from the heat. Place the eggs in a bowl, and immerse them in very cold water until cool. Remove the shells, then refrigerate the eggs until ready to use.

In a medium saucepan, bring about 2 cups water to a low boil. Peel the onions, and make a cross-cut in the top of each. Simmer the onions 10-12 minutes, or until translucent and pliable. Transfer the onions to a cutting board or flat dish. Using a shrimp fork or tomato carver, gently remove the very center of each bulb so that each onion becomes a small, hollow bowl.

In a small glass container, whisk the vodka and lemon juice. Add the onions, making sure that they are immersed in the vodka, then cover and refrigerate 2 hours.

When ready to serve, chop the eggs and arrange on a platter. Remove the onions from the vodka and place them on the egg. Fill each onion with 1 teaspoon of the sour cream and top with 1 teaspoon of the caviar. Garnish with lemon wedges and serve immediately.

*Serves 4-8*

*Note: If you like a stronger kick to your onion, simply chill for a longer period of time. For more citrus flavor, add lemon zest to taste.*

*Onions Vodka (recipe this page)*

# BETTINA'S ONION CAKE

**Dough**

1 package dry granulated
    yeast
½ cup milk, warmed to room
    temperature
2 cups bread flour
3 tablespoons butter
1 teaspoon salt
½ teaspoon freshly ground
    black pepper
1 teaspoon freshly grated
    lemon rind
1 teaspoon vegetable oil

**Topping**

4 slices cured bacon, diced
6 large Vidalia, Walla Walla, or
    other sweet onions, halved
    and thinly sliced
½ teaspoon freshly ground
    black pepper
4 eggs
1 cup sour cream
2 tablespoons caraway seeds
½ teaspoon salt
½ teaspoon freshly ground
    white pepper

*T*he people who live in the various geographic regions of Germany celebrate autumn with festivals that bring the countryside alive with dance, music, and food. Munich's Oktoberfest undoubtedly stands as the most popular of them all. Yet smaller villages and their families also come together to celebrate the harvest and enjoy special dishes created from the bounty of their farms and vineyards. My adopted German son Ralph and his family celebrate the season with apple wine and onion cake. This recipe finds its origins in the Palatinate region, where it's been a specialty for a few hundred years.

*For the dough*, in a small bowl, stir the yeast into the milk. Set aside 10-20 minutes, or until the milk has a layer of foam on top.

In a medium bowl, combine the flour, butter, salt, pepper, and lemon rind with a fork or pastry cutter. Add the yeast mixture, and stir until the dough is formed into a pliable ball. If the dough is too sticky to handle, add a little flour to your hands. Brush a large bowl with the oil, then transfer the dough to it. Cover with plastic wrap, and set aside in a warm, draft-free place 30-40 minutes, or until the dough has doubled in size.

*For the topping*, in a large frying pan, cook the bacon over medium heat until tender but not crisp. Lower the heat to medium-low, then add the onions and black pepper. Stirring often, cook 20 minutes, or until the onions are translucent and the liquid has evaporated.

Remove the pan from the heat and set aside.

In a medium bowl, mix the eggs, sour cream, caraway, salt, and white pepper, and set aside.

*To assemble*, on a floured surface, roll the dough to a thickness of ¼ inch. Place the dough on a greased 12-inch tart pan, pushing the dough up the sides. Spread the onions and bacon on top of the dough. Gently pour the egg mixture over the onion topping.

Preheat the oven to 375°F.

Allow the cake to rest 15 minutes, then bake, uncovered, 20-30 minutes, or until the liquid is set and the onions begin to brown. Remove the pan from the oven, and let it cool about 5 minutes before releasing the sides of the springform pan. Slice and serve.

*Yields ten 3-inch by 5-inch squares, or thirty-six 2-inch squares*

# SAGE LEAVES
# WITH LEMON-ANCHOVY DIP

1 large egg
¼ cup water
2 tablespoons minced fresh
   chives
½ teaspoon chopped fresh
   lemon thyme or lemon
   verbena
1 teaspoon grated Parmesan
   cheese
½ cup all-purpose flour
1 tablespoon virgin olive oil
2-3 cups peanut oil
60-70 large fresh sage leaves
Lemon-Anchovy Dip, 1 recipe

**Lemon-Anchovy Dip**
2 ounces flat anchovy fillets,
   drained and chopped
1 tablespoon fresh lemon juice

*A*lthough fried foods are not for those who want to watch fat *grams, these sage leaves are light enough to please even the most cautious palate. Serve them with a citrus vinaigrette, breadsticks, apples, or celery throughout the summer and into late fall. They're full of flavor without being stuffy.*

In a medium bowl, whisk the egg and water. Add the chives, lemon thyme, and cheese, mixing well. In another medium bowl, place the flour. Using a fork or an electric mixer at low speed, gradually blend in the egg mixture to form a smooth, slightly thick batter. Add the olive oil, blending until it is completely absorbed.

Pour the peanut oil into a deep, 8-inch to 10-inch frying pan or a medium saucepan. The oil should be about 1 inch deep. Heat to 350°F, or until the oil begins to bubble.

Dip each sage leaf into the batter, then onto wax paper. Fry 8-10 leaves at a time, 3-4 minutes, or until the leaves are golden and crisp. Remove the sage from the pan with a flat slotted spoon or chopsticks, then place on paper towels to drain. When all of the leaves have been fried, place them on a warm platter and serve immediately with the Lemon-Anchovy Dip.

*Serves 4-6*

*Note: Since these leaves are best when served hot, you may want to use two pans to fry everything at the same time. If doing so, remember to double the amount of peanut oil required.*

**Lemon-Anchovy Dip**
In a small bowl, mash the anchovies with a fork until they form a chunky paste. Add the lemon juice, blending with a fork or whisk. Cover and set aside in a cool place.

# PESTO RICOTTA TORTE

24 ounces ricotta cheese

½ cup grated Parmagiano-
Reggiano cheese

½ cup minced parsley

1 tablespoon extra-virgin
olive oil

1¼ pounds thin provolone
cheese slices, about
5 inches in diameter

Pesto Pesto, 1 recipe (see
page 158)

¾ cup sun-dried tomatoes
packed in olive oil, chopped

6-8 large opal or green basil
leaves, garnish

*P*esto Ricotta Torte offers a smooth yet zesty blend of herbs, garlic, and sun-dried tomato. The layers of red, white, and green also offer the palate a blend of compatible flavors and textures. Serve this colorful torte with crostini or Tuscany toast for a first course that satisfies a large group for dinner. Don't forget to serve a bottle of Frascati.

Allow the ricotta to warm up to room temperature 20 minutes, or until it is pliable with a fork. In a medium bowl, blend the ricotta, Parmagiano-Reggiano, and parsley. If you wish to make the ricotta mixture a day in advance of assembly, cover the bowl with plastic wrap and refrigerate until ready to use.

Brush a 5-inch by 9-inch oblong bread pan with the oil, or line it with plastic wrap. Line the sides, ends, and bottom of the pan with 8-10 slices of the provolone. Spoon one-half of the ricotta on the bottom of the pan, followed by one-half of the Pesto Pesto, then one-half of the tomatoes. Top with 2-3 provolone slices.

Continue to layer the remaining ricotta, Pesto Pesto, and tomatoes, then top with the remaining 3-4 slices of provolone. Cover with plastic wrap, and refrigerate 8-10 hours to allow the flavors to cure.

When ready to serve, remove the pan from the refrigerator, invert it onto a serving platter, and gently tap the sides and top with the handle of a butter knife. The torte will slide out of the pan easily. Garnish with top of the torte with basil.

*Serves 15-20*

*Note: This torte keeps well for several days in the refrigerator. For a smaller group of guests, you can simply halve the recipe.*

*Pesto Ricotta Torte*
*(recipe this page)*

# ROASTED SHALLOTS
# AND CIPOLLINI

8 large gray shallots
8 cipollini onions
one 4-inch sprig of fresh
  rosemary
two 4-inch sprigs of fresh
  thyme
½ cup virgin olive oil
⅓ cup water
¼ cup balsamic vinegar
1 teaspoon fine sea salt
½ teaspoon freshly ground
  black pepper

*Roasted shallots, like their garlic cousins, come with singular eating instructions. First, serve them hot or at room temperature. Pick them up one at a time with your fingers, then squeeze one end until the warm flesh pops into your mouth. Repeat this process as often as you like. Cipollini onions are bite-size and sweet. If they're not available from your grocer, a small sweet pearl onion can work for this recipe. However, the cipollini and shallots complement each other well.*

Preheat the oven to 375°F.

Clean the shallots by removing the stems and root ends with a paring knife. Make a small crosscut at the root end. Place the shallots and cipollini in a ceramic or earthenware casserole.

Remove the rosemary and thyme leaves from their stems, then place the leaves in a blender or food processor. Add the oil, water, vinegar, salt, and pepper. Blend at high speed 3-5 seconds, or until the ingredients are combined.

Pour the mixture over the shallots and cipollini, and toss gently with a spoon to make sure that all are coated. Cover and roast 40-45 minutes, or until the shallots and cipollini can be easily pierced with a cake tester or the tip of a knife.

Transfer to a warm baking dish and serve immediately.

*Serves 4*

*Note: This recipe doubles easily.*

# GARLIC-TARRAGON EGGS

8 large eggs
12 cloves mild garlic, peeled
3 teaspoons drained capers, rinsed
4 tablespoons extra-virgin olive oil
2 tablespoons chopped fresh tarragon
2 tablespoons chopped fresh basil
1 teaspoon white wine vinegar
salt and freshly ground black pepper, to taste
2 teaspoons freshly ground green peppercorns, garnish

*A number of cooks call tarragon the queen of herbs and find it indispensable in preparations for poultry, seafood, fish, vegetables, and grain dishes. When garlic and tarragon join for this egg dish, you'll enjoy an appetizer redolent with garlic and herbs that is easy to prepare. The eggs should chill for at least 1 hour before serving and can be prepared several hours in advance.*

Place the eggs and garlic in a medium saucepan, cover with water, and bring to a boil. Lower the heat to medium and simmer 10-12 minutes.

Take the eggs out of the saucepan and immerse them 5 minutes in a bowl of cold water. Remove the garlic from the saucepan and set aside to cool.

Drain the eggs, remove the shells, then slice the eggs in half lengthwise. Remove the yolks and place them in a small bowl or in a food processor. Add the garlic, capers, and oil. Blend with a mixer or food processor at medium-low speed until the ingredients form a chunky mixture. If using a food processor, transfer the mixture to a small bowl. Add the tarragon, basil, and vinegar, and stir by hand 1 minute, or until the ingredients are evenly combined. Season with salt and pepper.

Fill the egg white halves with the mixture and garnish with green pepper. Chill at least 1 hour before serving.

*Yields 16 egg halves; serves 8*

*Note: This recipe doubles easily for a buffet or a larger group of luncheon guests.*

# BAGNA CAUDA

2 ounces crostini
½ cup baby carrots
½ cup of 1-inch by 2-inch strips
    of red or yellow bell
    peppers
½ cup thinly sliced zucchini
2-3 stalks celery, cut into 2-inch
    to 3-inch pieces
¼ tablespoon virgin olive oil
2 tablespoons butter
6 cloves garlic, minced
½ can chopped anchovy filets
    packed in olive oil
¾ cup heavy cream

*W*arm bagna cauda *resounds with garlicky, anchovy-intense flavors that will either expand or reduce your circle of friends—that's what some people say. Yet this sauce repeatedly finds its way to tables in Italy, France, and the United States. This intense and simple starter apparently originated in Piemonte, Italy, only to cross European borders as well as oceans as its popularity grew. I prefer to serve it in cooler weather when the soul and the palate need a little extra warmth. Serve it with chunks of crusty bread and your favorite raw vegetables.*

Arrange the crostini, carrots, peppers, zucchini, and celery on a platter and set aside.

In a small saucepan, heat the oil and butter over medium heat until the butter is melted. Blend with a whisk, then add the garlic and anchovies with 2 teaspoons of their oil. Cook the mixture over low heat 5 minutes, using a wooden spoon to mash the garlic and anchovies as they cook. Blend in the cream with a whisk. Transfer the *bagna cauda* to a fondue pot or warming dish. Serve immediately.

*Yields 1¼ cups; serves 6-8*

Bagna Cauda (*recipe this page*)

# BALSAMIC CIPOLLINI
# AND MIXED BELLS

1 quart white wine vinegar
2½ cups water
⅓ cup extra-virgin olive oil
2 cloves rocambole garlic,
   minced
1 tablespoon coarse sea salt
¼ cup honey
½ teaspoon coarsely ground
   black pepper
½ cup chopped fresh opal basil
2 medium orange bell peppers
2 medium yellow bell peppers
2 medium red bell peppers
20 cipollini or small sweet
   onions, peeled
½ cup balsamic vinegar

*The flavor tip to this dish lies in making the balsamic mixture 4 days in advance of serving. This recipe doubles easily and keeps well in the refrigerator for up to 8 weeks. It can also be processed into pints for the winter months. Toss the balsamic cipollini and peppers with olives, chunks of fresh grilled tuna, and small boiled red potatoes for a feast.*

In a large saucepan, combine the wine vinegar, water, oil, garlic, salt, honey, black pepper, and basil. Bring the ingredients to a boil, then lower the heat and simmer 2-3 minutes.

Remove the stems and seeds from the peppers, then cut lengthwise into ½-inch strips. Peel the onions and make crosscuts at the stem ends. Add the peppers and onions to the saucepan, bring to a boil, and cook 3-4 minutes. Remove the vegetables with a slotted spoon and place them in 2 hot, clean quart jars.

Continue to boil the liquid another 5 minutes. Remove the pan from the heat, stir in the balsamic vinegar, then pour the liquid into the jars. Cover the jars tightly, allow them to stand until cool, and refrigerate.

*Yields 2 quarts*

*Note: In the jars, the vegetables should be completely immersed in liquid. If you run a little short, add more white wine vinegar.*

# SWEET ONION-OLIVE TAPENADE

½ cup chopped sweet red
  onions
½ cup chopped Vidalia, Walla
  Walla, or other sweet
  onions
1 cup drained, pitted, and
  chopped kalamata olives
3 cerignola olives, pitted and
  chopped
2 tablespoons drained capers,
  rinsed
2 tablespoons dry Marsala
  wine or dry vermouth
2 tablespoons extra-virgin
  olive oil
1 tablespoon chopped fresh
  parsley
1 tablespoon chopped fresh
  oregano
¼ teaspoon fresh lemon zest
1 clove garlic, crushed
freshly ground black pepper,
  to taste
balsamic vinegar, to taste
2 tablespoons finely chopped
  orange or red bell peppers
Chive-Parmesan Crostini,
  1 recipe (see page 97)

*While Vidalias and Walla Wallas are enjoyable without accompaniment, they also blend well with other onions, olives, and herbs. Combine onions, capers, and kalamata and cerignola olives for an appetizer that offers plenty of flavor without weighing you down. This tapenade is also a good side dish for a lunch of tossed greens, tangerines, and Country Onion Seed Bread (see recipe on page 103).*

Blend the onions, olives, and capers in a small bowl and set aside. Place the Marsala, oil, parsley, oregano, lemon zest, and garlic in a food processor. Pulse the mixture 3-5 seconds, then pour over the onion combination and blend with a fork. Transfer the mixture to a small serving dish, and season with black pepper and vinegar. Top with the bell peppers and serve with Chive-Parmesan Crostini.

*Yields 1½ cups*

# CARAMELIZED CIPOLLINI
# WITH BALSAMIC VINEGAR

35-40 cipollini onions
1¼ cups sugar
½ cup water
½ cup dry red wine
⅝ cup extra-virgin olive oil
1 cup red wine vinegar
1 cup white wine vinegar
¼ teaspoon salt
3-4 whole cloves
¼ cup balsamic vinegar
¼ teaspoon fresh lemon mint
    or lemon verbena, finely
    chopped

*Since cipollini are round and flat (like buttons) and can vary from ¾ inch to 1½ inches in diameter, the number that will fill a quart jar is never exact. You may want to purchase a few more than are called for. These onions need to steep in their marinade, so prepare them at least 3 days before serving. If you can't find cipollini, pearl onions make a tasty substitute, even though the balsamic blend is a better complement to cipollini.*

In a large stockpot, bring 4 quarts water to a boil. Make a crosscut at the root end of each onion, then drop the onions into the water and boil 1-2 minutes. Drain the onions in a colander, and rinse them under cold tap water. Once the onions are cool enough to handle, trim the stem end of each, allowing the outer skins to slip away easily. Leave the onions in the colander or transfer them to a bowl and set aside.

In a medium saucepan, bring the sugar and water to a boil, stirring continuously, until the mixture is a pale caramel color. Remove the pan from the heat, and pour in the red wine, continuing to stir. Add the oil, wine vinegars, salt, and cloves. Boil over medium-high heat 2-3 minutes, then add the onions. Cover the pot and simmer over medium heat 10-12 minutes. Remove the pan

from the heat, and add the balsamic vinegar and lemon mint, blending them into the mixture with a slotted spoon.

Remove the onions from the pan, and place them in a clean quart jar or two pint jars, until they reach about 1 inch from the top. Pour the liquid over the onions until they are completely covered. Cover and refrigerate at least 3 days. To serve, place the onions and a little of the marinade in a shallow dish and serve with toothpicks.

*Yields 1 quart*

*Note: Another serving suggestion is to wrap a little prosciutto ham around each onion and secure with tooth-picks. These onions keep well in the refrigerator for up to a month.*

# GRILLED TORPEDOES

### Dressing
3 leaves green basil
3 leaves opal basil
1 jalapeño or fresno chile, seeded and deveined
1 cup extra-virgin olive oil
½ teaspoon salt

### Torpedoes
8 Torpedo onions, peeled and cut in half lengthwise
4 cloves garlic, minced
one 4-ounce can diced chiles, drained (½ cup)
1 teaspoon *epazote*, oregano, or savory
¼ teaspoon ground red pepper
½ cup sour cream
1 cup shredded Monterey Jack cheese
½ teaspoon salt
½ teaspoon freshly ground black pepper
2 tablespoons lime juice
¼ cup olive oil

*W*hile this recipe calls for grilling these long, red, bottle-shaped onions, you could also bake them in the oven at 375°F. These onions aren't exceptionally long keepers, but they store successfully for several weeks after the harvest and make a grilled treat during the chillier days of late October and November. This recipe calls for epazote, *an herb that offers a distinctive flavor to Mexican cuisine. Some say that enjoying* epazote *is an acquired taste, so if it's not to your liking, try fresh oregano or winter savory instead.*

*For the dressing,* combine the basils, chile, oil, and salt in a blender, and process until smooth. Transfer to a small bowl and set aside.

*For the Torpedoes,* with a fork or the tip of a knife, gently remove some of the center flesh from each onion half to create a hollow shell. Dice the flesh that has been removed and set aside.

In a medium bowl, mix together the garlic, chiles, *epazote,* red pepper, and sour cream. Add the cheese and blend into the other ingredients. Add the salt and pepper and blend.

In a small bowl, whisk together the lime juice and oil, then brush some of this mixture on the insides of the Torpedoes. Stir the rest of this mixture with the diced onions.

With a spoon, fill the Torpedoes with the cheese mixture and top with the diced onion mixture. Drizzle the Torpedoes with some of the dressing.

Place the Torpedoes in an aluminum foil-lined baking pan. Grill over high heat 20-25 minutes, or until the Torpedoes can be easily pierced with the tip of a knife. Baste the Torpedoes with more of the dressing, and grill another 2-3 minutes. Serve immediately.

*Serves 4-8*

*Note: If you have some of the diced onion mixture left over, cover and reserve it for another use—marinated onions are delicious in fajitas and a variety of other Mexican dishes.*

# Salads and Side Dishes

*Acorn Squash Supreme*
*(recipe on page 74)*

# ACORN SQUASH SUPREME

2 acorn squash, cut in half
    lengthwise and seeded
2 Rome apples, cored and
    chopped with skins
2 tablespoons finely chopped
    leeks
¼ cup brown sugar
¼ cup pecan pieces
1½ teaspoons crushed fennel
    seeds
¼ cup orange juice
¼ cup melted butter
1 tablespoon shredded orange
    zest
½ teaspoon ginger

*S*quash and apples blend together easily and enhance turkey, chicken, lean pork, or bratwurst. It makes for a tasty foil to the recipe for Herb Crusted Turkey with Leek Stuffing (see page 120) and can often be found on the table at my house during Thanksgiving. (Photo on page 72.)

Preheat the oven to 375°F.

Place the squash cut side up in an ovenproof glass baking dish and add ¼ inch water.

In a large bowl, combine the apples, leeks, brown sugar, pecans, fennel seeds, orange juice, butter, orange zest, and ginger until well blended. Spoon the mixture evenly into the squash halves and cover loosely with aluminum foil.

Bake 35-45 minutes, or until the squash is easily perforated with the tip of a fork and the apple mixture is tender. Serve immediately.

*Serves 4*

*Note: The stuffing ingredients yield about 1¼ cups. You may have extra stuffing, depending upon the size of the squash and apples used. I bake the extra stuffing in the bottom of the pan along with the squash.*

# RENE'S SPRING HARVEST SALAD

1 clove garlic
2 cups mesclun
2 cups young green-leaf
   lettuce
1 cup baby beet greens
1 cup young endive or chicory
4 scallions, green and white
   parts, or green garlic stems,
   chopped
1 cup chopped, seeded
   cucumbers
4 ounces mild white goat
   cheese, cut into bite-size
   pieces
1 medium sweet red onion, cut
   into ⅛-inch slices
Tarragon Vinaigrette, 1 recipe
   (see page 157)
3 hard-boiled eggs, shelled
   and chopped
½ cup fresh red raspberries

*B*aby mixed greens and green garlic or young scallions bring a *refreshing touch of springtime to the kitchen table. This salad, along with Onion Rolls (see recipe on page 93) and sliced pears, creates a satisfying medley. Or enjoy it with fresh grilled tuna or game hen and a good bottle of Riesling for dinner. Many thanks to Rene Weyant, who made this salad a gem for the camera. (Photo on page 150.)*

Rub the sides and bottom of a wooden salad bowl with the garlic. Rinse, drain, and tear the mesclun, green-leaf lettuce, beet greens, and endive into pieces. Place the greens, scallions, and cucumbers in the salad bowl and toss. Gently toss in the goat cheese. Add the onions. Drizzle the Tarragon Vinaigrette over the salad and toss lightly. Add the eggs and toss lightly. Top the salad with the raspberries and serve immediately.

*Yields 7 cups; serves 6*

*Note: The Tarragon Vinaigrette can be made several hours or a day in advance of final assembly.*

# LEEK AND FENNEL
# WITH FRESH BASIL

2 tablespoons virgin olive oil

1 clove elephant garlic, finely chopped

2 cups sliced leeks

2 cups sliced or chopped fresh fennel

salt and freshly ground black pepper, to taste

¼ cup fresh Genovese basil

1 tablespoon balsamic vinegar

*T*he leek offers romance to nearly all it touches. Its gentle, sweet flavor along with the aromatic and lightly licorice flavor of the fennel blend to please the palate as a side dish to poultry and a variety of fish. It is also good with lamb roasted with garlic and mint. This dish makes for an elegant lunch when served with small, new red boiled potatoes, slices of creamy mild Cheddar, and fresh apple wedges.

In a large frying pan, heat the oil over medium heat. Sauté the garlic 3 minutes. Lower the heat to medium-low, then add the leeks and cook 7 minutes, or until the leeks begin to turn translucent. Add the fennel, season with salt and pepper, and cook 10-12 minutes, or until the fennel is tender. Transfer the vegetables to a serving bowl, and toss in the basil. Toss with the vinegar and serve immediately.

*Yields 1½ cups; serves 2*

*Leek and Fennel with Fresh Basil*
*(recipe this page)*

# ORANGE AND BEET SALAD

1 large clove garlic

2 large Valencia oranges, peeled and cut into bite-size pieces

16 ounces canned whole pickled baby beets, drained and cut in half

½ cup pitted and drained kalamata olives

⅓ cup extra-virgin olive oil

1½ tablespoons finely chopped fresh oregano

¼ teaspoon salt

¼ teaspoon freshly ground black pepper

*W*hen I tell people that I traditionally eat orange and beet salad with my supper on Christmas Eve, I watch their eyebrows rise a little closer to their hairlines. However unlikely this combination may seem, it's delicious and offers a palate-cleansing addition when served with stuffed, baked calamari, fried baby smelt, and capellini graced with marinara sauce. And, of course, there's the garlic bread and Chianti. If mention of the salad receives a strange response, I don't even begin to talk about the calamari—or the fact that its tentacles are used to flavor the pasta sauce. (Photo on page 118.)

Rub the sides and bottom of a medium wooden salad bowl with the garlic. Place the oranges, beets, olives, oil, and oregano in the bowl and toss until all of the ingredients are blended. Add the salt and pepper, toss again, and refrigerate 30 minutes before serving.

*Yields 3½ cups; serves 4-6*

*Note: If whole pickled beets are hard to find, quartered beets also work well. Sliced beets are not recommended, since they tend to break up when tossed.*

# GREEN GARLIC, RED ONION, ZUCCHINI CASSEROLE

1 cup mayonnaise

2 eggs

½ cup grated Parmagiano-Reggiano cheese

½ teaspoon salt

¼ teaspoon freshly ground white pepper

5 cups zucchini, cut into ⅛-inch-thick slices

½ red bell pepper, diced

1 cup diced red onions

½ cup chopped green garlic

⅓ cup minced fresh parsley

½ cup plain dry breadcrumbs

2 tablespoons butter

*T*his medley of onions, bell peppers, and zucchini enhances grilled meats, poultry, and fish. This recipe takes relatively little time and wins smiles from those who vow that they don't eat zucchini. You can enjoy this dish all year long, but it's best in mid- to late-summer when corn is perfect for roasting, onions are curing, and tomatoes are bursting with flavor.

Preheat the oven to 350°F.

In a small bowl, blend the mayonnaise, eggs, cheese, salt, and white pepper. Place the zucchini, peppers, onions, garlic, and parsley in a 2-quart, oiled casserole dish. Pour the mayonnaise mixture over the vegetables, and stir with a spoon until all ingredients are combined. Sprinkle the bread-crumbs on top of the mixture, and dot with the butter.

Bake 30-40 minutes, or until the casserole is bubbly and light golden brown. Remove from the oven and set aside 5-7 minutes to allow the casserole to set. Serve warm.

*Serves 4-6*

*Note: Although this dish is best fresh, it does keep well in the freezer 2-3 months.*

# ROASTED BELLS, GARLIC, AND BEL PAESE

1 head garlic, garnish
2 large red bell peppers
2 large yellow bell peppers
1 clove elephant garlic, peeled
    and minced
⅓ cup olive oil
1 teaspoon salt
¼ teaspoon ground cloves
juice of ½ lemon
6 slices Bel Paese cheese,
    1 inch in diameter and
    ¼ inch thick, or Cosa di
    Roma cheese
½ cup mixture of opal and
    green basil, garnish

*A platter of roasted peppers is almost impossible to resist, particularly when it's topped with creamy Bel Paese cheese. These peppers can accompany a tossed green salad and crusty bread for lunch. I also serve it with a variety of pasta dishes or risotto, since the combination of red and yellow peppers enhances the creamy glow of the cooked grains.*

Preheat the oven to 350°F.

Break the garlic into cloves and roast covered in an ovenproof baking dish 20-30 minutes. Remove from the oven, then when the garlic is cool enough to handle, gently squeeze the cloves out of their skins. Cut the cloves in half vertically and set aside.

Increase the oven temperature to 450°F. Place the peppers, with their stems intact, on a baking sheet or in a roasting pan, and roast 20-30 minutes, or until the skins darken and blister. Remove the peppers from the oven, and place them in a plastic bag. Close the bag and secure with a wire twist or a knot. Set the peppers aside to cool.

Place the elephant garlic, oil, salt, cloves, and lemon juice in a blender and mix 2-3 minutes, or until the mixture becomes a smooth sauce. Pour into a small bowl.

Take the peppers from the plastic bag, and remove the skins, stems, and seeds. If necessary, rinse the peppers to make peeling easier. Cut the peppers into vertical quarters and arrange on a serving dish. Top with the cheese. Whisk the oil mixture 1 minute, then pour over the peppers and cheese. Garnish with basil and the garlic. Serve immediately.

*Serves 4-6*

*Note: For added flavor, serve kalamata or green cerignola olives on the side. Olives also enhance the visual presentation of this dish.*

*Roasted Bells, Garlic, and Bel Paese (recipe this page)*

# CABBAGE ROTE

½ cup dry cured or regular
   bacon pieces
2 smoked ham shanks
1 head red cabbage, coarsely
   shredded
3 Jonathan or Rome apples,
   cored and chopped
2 large white winter onions,
   chopped
1 cup water
¾ cup red currant jelly
2 bay leaves
1 teaspoon salt
1 teaspoon freshly ground
   black pepper
½ cup apple cider vinegar

*While recipes for red cabbage prepared according to German tradition abound, this one remains a favorite. Serve it with bratwurst or your favorite beef roast along with boiled potatoes and warm, chunky applesauce. I traditionally make this along with sauerbraten, potatoes, and an apple dish for my German husband's birthday dinner, which occurs about the same time as Oktoberfest. But you don't need to be German to enjoy the harvest goodness in this dish.*

In a medium stockpot, sauté the bacon pieces 10 minutes over medium-low heat. Add the ham shanks, and cook another 10 minutes, turning to heat all sides. Add the red cabbage, apples, onions, water, jelly, bay leaves, salt, and pepper. Bring the mixture to a boil over medium-high heat, then reduce the heat to medium, cover, and simmer 1¼ hours, or until the ingredients are blended. Take out the bay leaves and stir in the vinegar. Cook the mixture 5 minutes, then transfer to a serving dish and serve immediately.

*Serves 6-8*

*Note: The ham shanks can be removed or served along with the red cabbage according to your preference. This recipe is good for canning and will retain color and flavor up to 6 months in the pantry. If you want to do some canning, remove the ham shanks, fill pint jars, and process in a pressure cooker or boiling-water bath, following instructions for your altitude.*

# POTATOES WITH GARLIC, LIME, AND CHILE

2 pounds new red potatoes,
    cut into 1¼-inch cubes
½ teaspoon salt
3 tablespoons virgin olive oil
6 cloves garlic, minced
3 tablespoons lime juice
1½ cups chopped scallions or
    bunching onions
1 cup chopped fresh flat-leaf
    parsley
1 cup chopped fresh cilantro
½ teaspoon salt
½ teaspoon freshly ground
    black pepper
1 teaspoon ground dried
    mirasol or other medium-
    hot chile
1½ teaspoons paprika
grated queso fresco or
    Parmesan cheese, garnish

*While this recipe can enhance your table throughout the year, savor it in September when chiles, garlic, and potatoes come forth so generously from the garden. The use of fresh-picked ingredients creates a healthy dish that can be served hot or at room temperature. Try serving this dish with grilled barbecued ribs, chicken, or salmon with grilled onions. This recipe also doubles easily when you want to serve a larger number of guests.*

Place the potatoes in a medium saucepan, add the salt, and cover the potatoes with water. Bring to a boil, then lower the heat to medium and simmer about 15 minutes, or until the potatoes are cooked but still firm.

While the potatoes are cooking, heat the oil, garlic, and lime juice over medium heat in a small saucepan.

Drain the potatoes, leaving them in the saucepan over low heat. Add the garlic mixture, and mix to coat the potatoes. Add the scallions, parsley, cilantro, salt, pepper, chile, and paprika, and gently blend into the potato mixture. If desired, garnish with cheese. Serve immediately.

*Yields 7 cups; serves 6*

# WARM ONION-MOZZARELLA SALAD

3 large red onions
8 slices fresh mozzarella
  cheese, ¼ inch thick
2 tablespoons virgin olive oil
2 tablespoons butter
1 yellow or orange bell pepper,
  chopped
2 tablespoons chopped fresh
  chives
2 tablespoons chopped fresh
  parsley
½ teaspoon salt
¼ teaspoon freshly ground
  white pepper
¼ cup hazelnuts, roasted,
  hulled, and halved
½ cup chopped fresh sorrel
balsamic vinegar, to taste

*T*he flavor of broiled or grilled red onion along with the herbs and creamy texture of fresh mozzarella make this a sumptuous side or main luncheon salad when served with fresh bread and grilled tuna. It's easy to assemble and gains a friendly tang from the inclusion of fresh sorrel. This salad has become an April tradition at my house, when the first young leaves of sorrel announce that spring has finally arrived.

Cut the onions into half-moon slices of about ½ inch, then arrange the slices on a baking sheet. Broil about 5 minutes, or until the skins begin to char. Remove from the broiler and set aside to cool.

Arrange the cheese slices on a serving platter, cover with plastic wrap, and refrigerate.

In a large frying pan, heat the oil and butter over low heat until the butter has melted. Increase the heat to medium, then add the peppers and sauté 7-10 minutes, or until the peppers begin to turn translucent. Add the onions, chives, parsley, salt, and white pepper, and mix with a spoon. Add the hazelnuts and sorrel, mix briefly, and remove from the heat.

Remove the cheese from the refrigerator, and spoon the mixture over the slices. Season with vinegar and serve immediately.

*Serves 4-6*

*Warm Onion-Mozzarella Salad*
*(recipe this page)*

# BRAISED TURNIPS, CARROTS, AND ONIONS

½ cup olive oil
1 tablespoon medium-dry
  sherry or dry vermouth
½ cup chopped lean bacon
1½ cups Vidalia, Walla Walla,
  or other sweet onions
½ cup chopped fresh chives
2 cloves red garlic, chopped
1 pound carrots, peeled and
  sliced
1 pound white turnips, peeled
  and cut into small cubes
¼ cup chopped fresh flat-leaf
  parsley
1 tablespoon chopped fresh
  thyme
½ cup chicken broth
1 tablespoon balsamic vinegar
½ teaspoon salt
½ teaspoon freshly ground
  green peppercorns

*Although this combination can be served as a side dish, you could also try it as a main dish by serving it with long-grain and wild rice with warm applesauce on the side. I call it comfort food and make it regularly once frost has chilled the air. Although this recipe calls for quite a bit of slicing and chopping, the results are well worth the effort.*

In a medium frying pan, heat the oil and sherry over low heat 3 minutes. Add the bacon, onions, chives, and garlic. Sauté and stir over medium heat until the onions become translucent. Add the carrots, turnips, parsley, and thyme, and blend into the onion mixture.

Add the broth, cover, and cook 20 minutes, or until the carrots and turnips are tender. Remove the pan from the heat, then add the vinegar, salt, and pepper, and stir into the vegetables. Transfer to a warm dish and serve immediately.

*Yields 5½ cups; serves 4-6*

# HARVEST BEET AND ONION SALAD

3 medium fresh red beets

3 medium fresh orange-gold beets

1 cup chopped Walla Walla, Vidalia, or other sweet onions

½ cup chopped fresh chives

¼ teaspoon chopped garlic

⅔ cup chopped fresh flat-leaf parsley

1 teaspoon chopped fresh lemon mint

½ teaspoon salt

½ teaspoon freshly ground black pepper

2 tablespoons white wine vinegar

¼ cup extra-virgin olive oil

*Beets that blush with hues of red and orange combine to resemble an afternoon sunset in August. However, the colors can continue to offer beauty to the table throughout the fall and into winter, since beets do store well under proper conditions. Although this recipe calls for chilling the salad before serving, I also enjoy it when the beets are still slightly warm.*

In a medium stockpot, bring 2 quarts water to a boil. Trim all but 2 inches of stalk from the beets, then drop the beets into the water. Simmer over medium-high heat 30-45 minutes, or until tender.

Remove the beets from the pot and allow them to cool. Remove the skins from the beets, cut off the remaining stalks, and cut the beets into ¾-inch cubes.

Place the beets, onions, chives, garlic, parsley, and lemon mint in a medium bowl and toss. Add the salt, pepper, vinegar, and oil, then toss again until all of the ingredients are coated.

Cover and refrigerate 2 hours. Remove the salad from the refrigerator, and allow it to sit uncovered 15 minutes before serving.

*Yields 5 cups; serves 6-8*

# GINGER BAKED ONIONS

½ pound coarsely ground
   country sausage
6 large Vidalia or mild winter-
   storage onions
2 medium Jonathan apples,
   cored and chopped
½ cup grated imported
   Gruyère cheese
¼ cup unfiltered organic apple
   juice
1 tablespoon orange juice
1 tablespoon ground ginger
½ teaspoon sage
¼ teaspoon salt
¼ teaspoon freshly ground
   white pepper

*Onions occupy center stage in this dish, and their sweetness is balanced by the apples and other ingredients to create a very flavorful yet digestible side to poultry, beef, and pork. Add a salad of tossed greens and mandarin oranges, sliced Emmentaler cheese, and a medium-dry red table wine for a simple, satisfying, and comforting supper with friends. The ingredients can be assembled a day in advance, allowing you to stuff and bake the onions along with the rest of dinner.*

In a small frying pan, brown the sausage gently over low heat 20 minutes. Remove the sausage from pan with a slotted spoon, place in a small bowl, and set aside to cool. Refrigerate the sausage if you plan to assemble the remaining ingredients more than 2 hours after cooking it.

Bring 2 quarts water to a slow boil in a medium saucepan. Peel the onions and make a crosscut at the top of each. Drop the onions into the water, and simmer, covered, 10-12 minutes. Transfer the onions to a colander, allowing them to drain thoroughly 10 minutes.

Preheat the oven to 375°F.

In a large bowl, combine the sausage, apples, cheese, juices, ginger, sage, salt, and white pepper until well blended. Set aside.

With a fork or paring knife, gently remove the center core of each onion (you can reserve the core for another use). Place the onions in an oiled ovenproof baking dish, arranging them so that they are touching each other. Gently spoon some of the sausage-apple mixture into each onion until it forms a mound on top. Bake loosely covered with foil 30 minutes, or until the cheese is bubbly and golden brown. Serve immediately.

*Serves 6*

*Note: While Vidalia onions are delicious prepared this way, milder winter-storage onions make handy substitutes during the colder months when Vidalias and other sweet, non-keeper onions aren't in season.*

*Ginger Baked Onions
(recipe this page)*

# Breads

The Flatbread Red Onion
Sandwich (recipe on page 92)

# THE FLATBREAD
# RED ONION SANDWICH

2 pita or flatbread rounds
½ cup Pesto Pesto (see
    page 158)
½ red or purple onion, thinly
    sliced
6 ounces shredded fontina
    cheese
balsamic vinegar, to taste

*Pita, or flatbread, began in kitchens throughout the Mediterranean countries and resides as a delicious diet staple today. Since grains are such an important part of the daily diet, pita can be found at nearly every meal. While pita offers an important addition to soups, stews, vegetable dishes, and meat dishes, it also translates well into sandwich fare. This recipe combines the grain with the pungency of pesto, red onions, and fontina cheese. (Photo on page 90.)*

Preheat the oven to 375°F.

Slice the pitas in half horizontally. Spoon equal amounts of the Pesto Pesto over the bottom halves. Add layers of onions, then cheese. Drizzle vinegar over the cheese, and cover with the top halves of the pitas.

Bake, uncovered, on a baking stone or sheet 12-15 minutes, or until the cheese melts and bubbles and the top crust looks golden brown. Remove from the oven, cut in half, and serve hot.

*Serves 2-4*

# ONION ROLLS

3 tablespoons dried onion
   flakes
1 cup boiling water
4 tablespoons softened butter
1½ teaspoons salt
2 tablespoons sugar
¼ teaspoon ground ginger
¼ cup warm water
1 package active dry yeast
   (2½ teaspoons)
1 egg, beaten
2 tablespoons dried dill weed
1 tablespoon chopped fresh
   chives
½ teaspoon crushed fresh
   rosemary
3 cups flour

*For centuries, the Jesuits have been recognized as masters of bread baking. Brother Richard Curry S.J. is no exception. He is the founder of the National Theater Workshop for the Handicapped, a teacher, and an extraordinary bread baker. In his cookbook,* The Secrets of Jesuit Bread Baking, *80 recipes and a variety of stories entertain the senses. This recipe for onion rolls is just a sample of baked goods that satisfy the palate while feeding the soul. (Photo on page 118.)*

In a small saucepan, add the onion flakes to the water, cover, and set aside 20 minutes.

In a large bowl, combine the butter, salt, and sugar.

Drain the onion flakes, then set the flakes aside and bring the reserved liquid to a gentle boil. Pour the liquid into the butter and sugar mixture. Stir until the sugar is dissolved. Set the mixture aside to cool to lukewarm.

In a small bowl, combine the ginger, warm water, and yeast, stirring until the yeast dissolves. Add to the butter mixture, and stir to combine the ingredients. Add the egg, onion flakes, dill, chives, and rosemary, blending with a fork. Gradually add the flour until a dough forms and begins to pull away from the sides of the bowl.

Place the dough in a large, lightly oiled bowl and turn to coat all sides with oil. Cover with plastic wrap and refrigerate 45 minutes.

Preheat the oven to 350°F. Grease a muffin tin.

Remove the dough from the refrigerator and punch it down. Fill each muffin cup one-third to one-half full with the dough. Cover the tin with a kitchen towel and allow the dough to rise in a warm, draft-free place 45 minutes.

Once the dough has nearly doubled in size, bake 20-25 minutes, or until the tops of the muffins turn golden brown. Transfer the muffin tin to a wire rack to cool. Wait until the tin is almost completely cool before removing the muffins. The muffins will still be slightly warm and ready to serve.

*Yields twelve 3-inch muffins or eighteen 2½-inch muffins*

*Note: This recipe doubles easily and the muffins freeze well, so you may want to bake enough to serve immediately and to freeze for the future.*

# PIZZA WITH CRAB, ONIONS, AND BELL PEPPERS

## Dough
1 cup warm water
½ teaspoon sugar
1 package dry yeast
  (2½ teaspoons)
3-4 cups bread flour
2 teaspoons salt
2 tablespoons butter, chipped
2-3 tablespoons olive oil

## Topping
1½ cups fresh crabmeat,
  thoroughly drained
3-4 drops Tabasco
1 cup chopped Vidalia onions
1 teaspoon lemon juice
½ teaspoon freshly ground
  white pepper
1 tablespoon garlic powder
1½ cups shredded mozzarella
  cheese
½ cup grated Parmagiano-
  Reggiano cheese
1 roasted red or orange bell
  pepper, peeled, seeded,
  and cut into ½-inch-wide
  strips
1 roasted yellow bell pepper,
  peeled, seeded, and cut
  into ½-inch-wide strips

*P*izza *often provokes curious cooks to experiment with different flavors. While seafood and cheese are known to be unlikely companions, this combination along with the zest of onions and peppers somehow works.*

*For the dough,* place the water in a small bowl. Add the sugar and whisk until dissolved. Add the yeast, blending gently into the water. Set aside in a warm place 10 minutes, or until a layer of foam forms on top.

In a large bowl, combine 3 cups of the flour with the salt and butter pieces. Blend the butter into the flour with your fingertips. Add the yeast mixture, blending it into the flour with a fork until enough liquid is absorbed so that the dough can be kneaded. Add more flour if necessary.

Turn the dough onto a floured surface and knead 5-10 minutes, adding more flour if necessary. The dough should be smooth, shiny, and soft. Put the oil a large bowl, then turn the dough in the oil to coat on all sides. Cover with plastic wrap, and let the dough rise 45 minutes, or until it doubles in size.

Preheat the oven to 375°F.

Roll out the dough to a thickness of ⅜ inch, then place it in an oiled 17-inch by 11-inch by 1-inch baking pan or on a similar size baking stone.

*For the topping,* combine the crabmeat, Tabasco, onions, lemon juice, white pepper, and garlic powder in a medium bowl.

Cover the dough with ½ cup of the mozzarella, then the Parmagiano-Reggiano. Add the crab mixture, then the peppers. Top with the remaining mozzarella.

Bake 20-25 minutes. Remove the pizza from the oven, and serve immediately.

*Serves 8-12*

*Note: The peppers can be roasted and set aside or refrigerated a day in advance of the pizza preparation.*

*Pizza with Crab, Onions, and Bell Peppers (recipe this page)*

# GREEN GARLIC, SUN-DRIED TOMATO, ROSEMARY BREAD

1 package active dry yeast (2½ teaspoons)

2 tablespoons sugar

1 tablespoon salt

3½-4 cups white bread flour

½ cup hot water

2 large eggs

1 stick butter, cut into ¼-inch slices

½ cup washed, drained, and chopped sun-dried tomatoes

½ cup finely chopped green garlic

1 tablespoon chopped fresh rosemary

1 egg yolk beaten with 1 tablespoon warm water

*T*he combination of rosemary and tomato offers a slightly heady touch to zucchini, pasta, and rice. It also creates a bread that complements a variety of soups, sandwiches, and cheeses. Try this bread with potato-leek soup or with a salad of fresh basil, grilled tuna, and green olives for a healthy, balanced lunch. Herbs, especially basil and rosemary, can make any dish lighten up and dance on your tongue. (Photo on page 109.)

In a large bowl, combine the yeast, sugar, salt, and 1 cup of the flour until well blended. Stir in the water with a fork. Blend in the eggs until they are completely absorbed. Add the butter, working it into the mixture with the fork until it is evenly distributed. Add 2½ cups of the flour gradually, kneading it into the mixture. Combine the tomatoes, garlic, and rosemary in a small bowl, then add to the flour mixture.

Knead the dough 5-10 minutes, or until smooth and somewhat glossy. Since the dough tends to be a little sticky, add more flour until the dough pulls away from the sides of the bowl and no longer clings to your fingers.

Turn the dough out onto a floured board or work surface and knead another 5 minutes. Place the dough in a large, lightly oiled bowl and turn to coat all sides with oil. Cover the bowl with plastic wrap,

and set aside in a draft-free place to rise 1½ hours, or until the dough has doubled in size.

Preheat the oven to 375°F.

Punch down the dough, remove it from the bowl, and form it into a round loaf on a lightly floured work surface. Transfer the dough to a baking stone and brush the top with the egg wash. (Instead of using a baking stone, you could also use a cake pan with the bottom greased.)

Bake 30-40 minutes, or until the bread is firm, golden, and easy to move on the stone. Remove from the oven and allow the bread to rest 10 minutes before transferring to a wire rack.

*Yields 1 loaf*

# CHIVE-PARMESAN CROSTINI

1 slender French baguette or crusty loaf of Italian bread
⅝ cup extra-virgin olive oil
1 tablespoon chopped fresh chives
1 French red shallot, preferably Frog's Leg, peeled and chopped
1 teaspoon grated Parmagiano-Reggiano cheese
⅛ teaspoon paprika

*C*rostini are so simple to make that it's easy to keep a can of them on hand. While they can be seasoned or baked plain, they add taste and crunch to appetizers, soups, and cheese. The addition of chives in this recipe enhances olives, onions, pumpkin, and squash.

Preheat the oven to 350°F.

Slice the bread into ¼-inch to ⅜-inch rounds. Place the rounds in a single layer on a baking sheet and set aside.

In a blender or food processor, combine the oil, chives, shallots, cheese, and paprika 10 seconds, or until the ingredients are well mixed. Pour into a small bowl. With a pastry brush, brush half of the chive-oil mixture onto the bread rounds.

Bake on the middle rack of the oven 7-10 minutes. Turn the slices over, brush with the remaining chive-oil mixture, and bake another 7 minutes, or until golden.

Allow the crostini to cool to room temperature, then serve or place in an airtight container for future use.

*Yields 36 crostini*

# ONION CUSTARD CORNBREAD

1 tablespoon peanut oil

2 eggs, at room temperature

3 tablespoons melted butter, cooled

2 tablespoons sugar

2 cups whole milk

2 tablespoons white vinegar

1 cup all-purpose flour

¾ cup yellow cornmeal

1 teaspoon baking powder

½ teaspoon baking soda

½ teaspoon salt

1 teaspoon chopped fresh oregano

½ teaspoon chopped fresh sage

½ cup golden raisins

⅓ cup seeded and minced jalapeño chiles

⅓ cup chopped mild yellow onions

1¼ cups heavy cream

*This cornbread-onion dish utilizes a variety of herbs, chiles, and other savory foods from the garden. This recipe blends jalapeños, onions, and golden raisins. Serve this cornbread for breakfast or brunch with eggs, fresh melons, berries, oranges, or your favorite sausage. I prefer the pungency of fresh onions and peppers in the early fall, when the harvest is at its peak.*

Preheat the oven to 375°F. Brush a 12-inch cast-iron skillet with the oil.

In a medium bowl, mix the eggs and butter with an electric hand mixer until the liquid becomes a creamy yellow color. Add the sugar, milk, and vinegar, then blend with the mixer another 2-3 minutes and set aside.

In a large bowl, combine the flour, cornmeal, baking powder, baking soda, and salt. Blend in the oregano, sage, and raisins with a large mixing spoon or fork.

Put the skillet into the oven and heat at least 5 minutes before baking the bread.

Gradually add the egg mixture to the flour mixture, mixing until smooth. Stir in the chiles and onions.

Slide the rack and skillet out of the oven. Pour the batter into the skillet, then pour the heavy cream in the middle of the batter. Bake 45-55 minutes, or until the top of the cornbread is firm and golden and the sides have pulled slightly away from the skillet. Transfer the skillet to a cake rack and allow the cornbread to cool 10 minutes before serving.

*Yields 1 loaf*

*Onion Custard Cornbread
(recipe this page)*

# THE RUSTIC ONION, HERB, TUNA SALAD SANDWICH

1 cup diced white globe onions
6 scallions, diced
6 stalks celery, diced
1 cup chopped fresh flat-leaf
  parsley
½ teaspoon granulated garlic
⅛ teaspoon paprika
1 tablespoon chopped fresh
  tarragon
1 pinch of freshly ground black
  pepper
salt, to taste
24 ounces solid-white, water-
  packed canned tuna,
  drained
1½-2 cups mayonnaise
12-16 slices Country Onion
  Seed Bread (see page 103)
6-8 teaspoons Dijon mustard
fresh tomato slices, to taste
alfalfa sprouts, to taste

*L*a Doce Vita Café in Colorado Springs, Colorado, offers nourishment *for the soul as well as for the body. Books and prints line the walls of the café that also houses poets, writers, and chess players. Tables, pencils, and paper offer sanctuary for the creative spirit while the café sends forth a number of delectables at breakfast and lunch. This recipe is an adaptation of the café's most popular sandwich. The tuna salad can be made in advance of final prep, and the substantial quantity provides an easily assembled lunch for a crowd.*

Place the onions, scallions, and celery in a medium bowl. Toss in the parsley until it is evenly distributed. Sprinkle the garlic, paprika, tarragon, pepper, and salt over the vegetables and blend into the mixture with a spoon. Blend in the tuna and 1½ cups of the mayonnaise. If the mixture is drier than you'd like, add more mayonnaise. Set aside or refrigerate for future use.

Toast the bread, then spread each of the bottom sandwich slices with 1 teaspoon mayonnaise and each of the top slices with 1 teaspoon mustard. Spoon some of the tuna salad on the slices brushed with mayonnaise. Place tomato slices and alfalfa sprouts on top of the tuna salad. Cap with the mustard-brushed slices. Serve immediately.

*Yields 7 cups tuna salad; serves 6-8*

# OLIVE AND ONION DEEP-DISH PIE

**Crust**
1 tablespoon salt
¾ cup vegetable shortening
⅓ boiling water
2-2½ cups bread flour
1 tablespoon chopped fresh
    tarragon

**Filling**
6 jumbo eggs
1½ cups heavy cream
2 cups finely chopped red
    globe onions
½ cup drained, sliced ripe
    olives
1 tablespoon chopped fresh
    chives
½ cup shredded imported
    Gruyère cheese
2 tablespoons freshly grated
    Romano cheese
¼ teaspoon ground nutmeg
½ teaspoon freshly ground
    white pepper

*O*lives, onions, herbs, and spices blend to offer a warming lunch or light supper throughout the colder months. The creamy custard doesn't contain much cheese, however the combination of eggs, heavy cream, and a seasoned crust creates a pie that is rich but not heavy. You can use a deep-dish pie plate or a shallow, oblong cake pan, depending upon your personal tastes. If you bake this quiche in an oblong pan, you can cut it into bite-size squares that can be served as an appetizer.

*For the crust,* place the salt and shortening in a medium bowl. Pour in the water, and blend with a fork or whisk until smooth. Add 2 cups of the flour and blend the mixture with a fork until the dough begins to form. If the dough feels too sticky, add a little more flour. Add the tarragon, blending into the dough by hand. Do not overwork the dough or it will be tough instead of light and flaky.

Roll out the dough between two pieces of waxed paper until it is ¼ inch thick. Transfer to a 10-inch deep-dish pie plate. Flute the edges, cover with waxed paper, and refrigerate until ready to fill.

Preheat the oven to 375°F.

*For the filling,* in a large bowl, whisk the eggs and cream until smooth and thick, then set aside. Remove the pie crust from the refrigerator. Spread the onions, olives, and chives on the bottom of the pie shell. Top with the cheeses. Whisk the nutmeg and white pepper into the egg mixture, then pour into the pie.

Bake 45-50 minutes, or until the crust is golden and the pie is set. Turn off the oven and open the door. Allow the pie to cool 15 minutes. Remove the pie from the oven, and allow it to set another 15 minutes before slicing. Serve warm.

*Serves 6-8*

*Note: The crust can be made 2-3 days ahead, then rolled out when you're ready for final assembly.*

# COUNTRY ONION SEED BREAD

3½ cups warm water
1 package active dry yeast
   (2½ teaspoons)
4 tablespoons sugar
7 cups unbleached bread flour
2 tablespoons salt
3 cups whole-wheat bread
   flour
1 cup fine yellow cornmeal,
   plus additional for dusting
   baking sheets
¼ cup onion seeds
¼ cup chopped fresh parsley
1 egg beaten with 3 tablespoons warm water
¼ cup sesame seeds

*O*nion seeds frequently occupy a seat in Eastern and Indian *dishes. They are easy to digest and lend a wonderful aroma as well as subtle yet lingering flavor to rice, lentils, and breads. The following recipe blends onions with parsley and sesame seeds in a dense and satisfying country bread. It makes excellent French toast, but you may want to omit the onion and sesame seeds.*

In a large bowl, combine 1 cup of the water with the yeast, 2 tablespoons of the sugar, and 2 cups of the unbleached flour. Cover and set aside in a draft-free place 20 minutes.

Once the yeast mixture has expanded, add the remaining water, sugar, and salt, blending the mixture with a fork. Add the remaining unbleached flour and whole-wheat flour gradually, working the dough to absorb each addition. Add the cornmeal, onion seeds, and parsley, and knead into the dough until blended.

Place the dough in a large, lightly oiled bowl and turn to coat all sides with oil. Cover with plastic wrap, and set in a draft-free place to rise 1½ hours, or until the dough has doubled in size.

Brush two baking sheets with oil and cover with a light layer of cornmeal. Uncover the dough and punch it down. Divide it in half and knead each half 5 minutes. Form the halves into two loaves, placing one on each baking sheet, and cover with a kitchen towel. Let the dough rise again in a draft-free place 30-45 minutes, or until the dough has nearly doubled in size.

Preheat the oven to 375°F.

Brush the top and sides of each loaf with the egg wash. With a sharp knife, cut a vertical slit down the center of each loaf and diagonal cuts on the sides. Sprinkle the top and sides of each loaf with the sesame seeds.

Bake 45-50 minutes. When done, the crust should be golden brown and the loaves should move easily on the baking sheets. Remove the loaves from the oven and allow them to sit 10 minutes before transferring to a wire rack to cool.

*Yields 2 loaves*

top: *Country Onion Seed Bread*
*(recipe this page);*
bottom: *Pasta* Puttanesca
*(recipe on page 124)*

# Soups and Stews

*Leek Harvest Soup*
*(recipe on page 106)*

# LEEK HARVEST SOUP

1 red bell pepper, garnish
3 quarts rich chicken broth
2 large baking potatoes,
    peeled and cut into chunks
3 large leeks, white parts,
    cleaned and chopped
1 cup chopped fresh flat-leaf
    parsley
2 tablespoons chopped fresh
    chives
1 tablespoon minced garlic
1 tablespoon chopped
    fresh dill
1 teaspoon salt
1 teaspoon freshly ground
    white pepper
2 tablespoons extra-virgin
    olive oil

*Fresh dill and parsley transform this leek and potato combination. Once parsley and dill reach their full flavor in the garden, make plenty of this soup for the colder months. It's delicious any time of year and provides a refreshing flavor even in warmer weather. It's full of vitamins, iron, and potassium, certainly enough to revive the body and rejuvenate the spirit. Make it a day in advance of serving for the best flavor. (Photo on page 104.)*

Preheat the oven to 450°F.

Place the pepper on a baking sheet and roast uncovered 30-40 minutes, or until the skin begins to char and blister. Place the pepper in a plastic bag, tie the bag at the top, and set aside to cool 20 minutes. Remove the stem, skin, and seeds from the pepper, then chop it, place in a small dish, cover, and set aside.

In a medium stockpot, bring the broth to a boil over medium-high heat. Add the potatoes and cook over medium heat 10-15 minutes, or until the potatoes are somewhat tender. Remove from the stove, then using a potato masher, break the potatoes to look like a thick, chunky pudding. Add the leeks, and return the pot to the stove. Cook 15 minutes over medium heat, then add the parsley, chives, garlic, dill, salt, white pepper, and oil. Lower the heat and simmer 30 minutes, stirring occasionally to prevent the mixture from sticking to the pot. Transfer to individual serving bowls, garnish with the peppers, and serve immediately.

*Yields 8 cups; serves 6-8*

*Note: This soup can be stored in the freezer without the roasted peppers 3 months. Add the peppers when ready to serve.*

# STIFADO

¼-⅓ cup olive oil

3 pounds sirloin tip, cut into 1-inch cubes

3 cups sliced sweet yellow onions

2 cups sliced mildly hot white onions

5 large cloves garlic, minced

1 tablespoon salt

1 teaspoon freshly ground green peppercorns

one 4-inch stick cinnamon

3 cups dry red table wine

one 16-ounce can tomato sauce

4 plum tomatoes, seeded and chopped

*Stifado hails from the Mediterranean, where the people of Mykonos, Athens, and their neighbors share an appreciation for unusual flavor combinations that result when different spices and herbs unite with vegetables and meat. This particular stew remains among the most aromatic at my table. The onions, cinnamon, and tomatoes create a mellow intensity that adds a unique dimension to the beef. Serve this stew with fresh pita bread, sliced cucumbers, and kalamata olives for a robust ethnic meal.*

In a large, cast-iron Dutch oven or enamel stockpot, heat the oil over medium heat. Gently brown the meat in batches, then remove from the pot and set aside.

Add the onions and garlic to the pot, and sauté over medium-low heat 5-7 minutes, or until the onions are slightly translucent. Add the salt, green pepper, cinnamon, wine, tomato sauce, and tomatoes, and bring the mixture to a boil. Add the meat and reduce to heat to low. Cover and simmer, stirring occasionally, 2 hours, or until the meat is tender when pierced with a fork. Remove the cinnamon stick. Serve hot.

*Yields 8 cups; serves 6-8*

*Note: This stew keeps well in the freezer 3-4 months.*

# MUSSELS MARINARA

1 tablespoon olive oil

3 red bell peppers, chopped

1 cup chopped leeks, white parts

4 large shallots, peeled and chopped

3 cloves garlic, chopped

one 28-ounce can chopped plum tomatoes

¾ cup Chianti wine

3 pounds mussels, cleaned and rinsed

1 cup bottled clam juice

1 cup water

½ cup tightly packed chopped fresh basil

½ cup chopped fresh parsley

2 tablespoons chopped fresh oregano

1 teaspoon fine sea salt

1 tablespoon freshly ground green peppercorns

*F*resh mussels, when steamed with wine, herbs, and tomatoes, create an open invitation for a feast. Add hot fresh bread, a light soave or zinfandel, and a few hungry people, and the stage is set. Since this stew contains a hearty blend of vegetables and seasonings, I even bypass a green salad. While dinner by the sea may not be an option, the mental traveler will surely sense and taste it here.

In a large stockpot or Dutch oven, heat the oil over medium-low heat. Cook the peppers, leeks, shallots, and garlic 5 minutes. Add the tomatoes and wine, then increase the heat to medium and cook 20 minutes. Add the mussels, clam juice, water, basil, parsley, and oregano. If the sauce seems a bit thick, add a little more water or clam juice.

Cover and simmer over medium-low heat 10-15 minutes, or until the mussels open. With a wooden spoon, blend in the salt and green pepper. Simmer 1 minute. Remove the stew from the heat, discard any unopened mussels, and serve immediately.

*Serves 4-6*

*Note: The sauce mixture, without the mussels, keeps well in the refrigerator up to 1 week. It can also be made ahead and put in the freezer, where it will keep up to 2 months. However, the flavor is most vibrant when the blend of herbs and seasonings is served fresh.*

*top: Green Garlic, Sun-Dried Tomato, Rosemary Bread (recipe on page 96); bottom: Mussels Marinara (recipe this page)*

# WILDLY STROGANOFF

1½ pounds top sirloin, cut into
2-inch strips
1 pound round steak, cut into
2-inch strips
1½ cups flour
¼ cup peanut oil
2 quarts Steeped Turkey or
Chicken Broth, at room
temperature
½ stick butter
½ cup medium-dry sherry
1 white winter onion, chopped
1 mild yellow onion, chopped
1 cup thinly sliced cremini
mushrooms
1 cup thinly sliced white
mushrooms
1 bay leaf
1 teaspoon sea salt
1 tablespoon coarsely ground
black pepper
1 tablespoon paprika
16 ounces sour cream

*Colder weather seems to ignite the desire for warm comfort food, and stroganoff with elegantly gracing wide egg noodles falls into that category. This recipe calls for a blend of meats, onions, and mushrooms. Serve it fresh or omit the sour cream and keep it in the freezer up to 3 months. Somehow, stroganoff that simply needs to be thawed and heated can take the edge off a cold and uncomfortable day. This recipe is especially good when made with Steeped Turkey or Chicken Broth, but you can substitute canned beef broth.*

Dredge the beef in the flour. In a large, cast-iron skillet, warm 1 tablespoon of the oil over medium heat. Gently brown the beef on all sides in batches, adding more of the oil before each batch. Set the beef aside, then deglaze the skillet with 1 cup of the Steeped Turkey or Chicken Broth, stirring to remove all of the brown pieces. Set aside.

In another large, cast-iron skillet, melt the butter over medium heat. Add the sherry, and cook, stirring constantly, 1 minute. Add the onions, and sauté 15 minutes, or until translucent and tender. Add the mushrooms, stirring to coat with the butter and sherry mixture. Cook the onions and mushrooms another 10 minutes, then remove the skillet from the heat. Remove the vegetables, then deglaze the skillet with 1 cup of the broth.

Place the beef, onions, and mushrooms in a casserole or Dutch oven, add the deglazing broth, and cook over medium heat 10 minutes. Add the remaining broth, bay leaf, salt, and pepper. Bring the mixture to a boil, then partially cover and simmer over low heat 30 minutes, or until the beef is fork tender. Stir in the paprika, and simmer another 5 minutes. Over very low heat, stir in the sour cream until all of the ingredients are blended. Serve immediately.

*Yields 5 cups; serves 8-10*

*Note: Serve this dish with wide egg noodles or a combination of long-grain and wild rice.*

**Steeped Turkey or Chicken Broth**

In a large stockpot, bring the water to a boil. Add the turkey and return to a gentle boil. Add the onion, carrot, celery, bay leaves, cinnamon, chiles, salt, and pepper, then simmer, partially covered, 15 minutes over medium heat. Tightly cover and turn off the heat. Allow the ingredients to steep 1¼ hours. Remove the turkey, place in a container, and refrigerate for another use. Strain the broth and discard the vegetables. Refrigerate the broth at least 8 hours, then skim off the fat. Use immediately or transfer to airtight containers and freeze for future use.

*Yields 4 quarts*

*Note: Since broth provides the basis for many soups, stews, and main dishes, it's always good to keep a quart or two on hand.*

5 quarts water
3 pounds turkey leg quarters, or one 3-pound chicken
1 large white globe onion
1 carrot
3 stalks celery, cut into 4-inch to 5-inch lengths
4 bay leaves
two 3-inch cinnamon sticks
2 dried pequin chiles
1 jalapeño chile, seeded
1 tablespoon salt
1 tablespoon freshly ground black pepper

# COUNTRY ONION SOUP

**Consommé**

½ cup chopped bacon

4 large beef bones with their meat

6 quarts hot water

2 carrots

3 large leeks, cleaned with green leaves removed

1 turnip

1 large white globe onion, pierced with 6 whole cloves

1 bay leaf

4 juniper berries

1 tablespoon coarse sea salt

1 teaspoon freshly ground black pepper

**Soup**

¼ cup olive oil

6 Walla Walla onions, halved and thinly sliced

1 cup chopped leeks, white parts

2 cloves elephant garlic, minced

½ cup medium-dry sherry

1 teaspoon salt

1 teaspoon freshly ground white pepper

6-8 slices Swiss Gruyère cheese

6-8 slices stale French bread

freshly ground black pepper, to taste

*Country Onion Soup
(recipe this page)*

*Y*ou can easily double this soup, so make large batches of consommé that can be used fresh or kept in the freezer. During the weeks that span August, September, and October, I make regular meals of soup, bread, sliced apples and pears, Emmentaler or Gruyère cheese, sweet pickles, and olives. Whether it's lunchtime or dinnertime, this soup makes sharing a meal with friends a very easy thing to do. If you don't want to make the consommé from scratch, you can substitute a rich canned variety.

*For the consommé*, in a large stockpot, gently brown the bacon over medium heat 10 minutes. Remove the bacon and set aside.

Place the beef bones in the pot and brown on all sides. Add the bacon and water, then bring to a boil over medium-high heat. Reduce the heat to medium-low, and add the carrots, leeks, turnip, onion, bay leaf, berries, salt, and pepper. Simmer 2 hours, or until the liquid is reduced by nearly half. Allow the consommé to cool completely, then refrigerate 8 hours or overnight.

Skim the fat from the consommé, pour into a separate container, and refrigerate until ready for use. Discard the vegetables.

*For the soup*, in a medium stockpot, heat the oil over medium heat. Sauté the onions, leeks, and garlic 15-20 minutes, or until the onions and leeks are tender and translucent. Add the sherry and cook over medium heat another 7 minutes. Add the 3 quarts consommé, salt, and white pepper. Simmer over low heat 15-20 minutes, or until the liquid is reduced by 1 inch.

While the soup is simmering, place a slice of cheese on each slice of bread. Sprinkle lightly with black pepper, then broil until the cheese turns golden brown and melts over the sides of the bread.

Place a slice of bread at the bottom of individual serving crocks. Ladle the soup over the bread and serve immediately.

*Yields 12 cups; serves 6-8*

*Note: If you don't care to make the consommé from scratch, combine two 14½-ounce cans of consommé with two cans of water to make 3 quarts of liquid.*

# GARLIC-SAGE SOUP

8 cups rich chicken broth
20 large sage leaves
15 cloves red garlic, chopped
1 large carrot, diced
2 tablespoons chopped fresh
   parsley
2 tablespoons snipped fresh
   chives
1 teaspoon salt
1 teaspoon crushed green
   peppercorns
¼ cup extra-virgin olive oil
6 eggs, optional
6 slices coarse, dry Italian or
   French bread, ½ inch thick
freshly grated Parmagiano-
   Reggiano cheese, garnish

*L*ong respected for their medicinal attributes, garlic and sage have been known to remedy flus, colds, and digestive disorders. They are one of many herb combinations that feed the body as well as the soul. It's no wonder that recipes for soups and teas calling for garlic and sage appear in kitchens all over the world. This recipe for garlic soup offers the option of floating a poached egg in each soup bowl. With or without the egg, this soup restores the body while pleasing the palate.

In a medium stockpot, bring the broth and sage to a boil. Lower the heat and simmer 15 minutes. Remove the sage and discard. Add the garlic, carrots, parsley, and chives, then cover and simmer over medium-low heat 20 minutes. Add the salt, green pepper, and oil, and simmer another 5 minutes. If desired, add the eggs and gently poach them in the broth about 5 minutes, or until they are fairly firm.

To serve, place a slice of bread at the bottom of each soup bowl. Add the broth to each bowl, then gently lift the eggs with a slotted spoon and add to each serving. Sprinkle with cheese and serve immediately.

*Yields 7 cups; serves 6*

*Note: Soup tends to cool quickly after leaving the soup pot. I recommend using earthenware or ovenproof serving crocks to keep the soup warm. While the soup can be made in the morning for supper, it tastes best when allowed to rest overnight. The broth keeps well in an airtight container in the refrigerator about 7 days and tastes best when reheated just one time.*

# PUMPKIN-LEEK SOUP

3 tablespoons virgin olive oil
3 cups chopped leeks, white
   parts
6 cups fresh pumpkin, cut into
   1-inch cubes
3 cups rich chicken or turkey
   broth
½ teaspoon ground cloves
½ teaspoon salt
½ teaspoon freshly ground
   black pepper
½ teaspoon grated lemon zest
1 cup whole milk
lemon juice, to taste

*Pumpkin-Leek Soup never fails to satisfy throughout the fall, winter, and early spring. It complements warm Onion Rolls (see page 93) or Onion Custard Cornbread (see page 98) for a healthy and energizing meal. You can substitute butternut squash for the pumpkin. I have even tried equal amounts of squash and pumpkin for an interesting and flavorful combination.*

In a medium saucepan, heat the oil over medium heat. Sauté the leeks until they are soft and slightly golden. Stir in the pumpkin, broth, cloves, salt, pepper, and lemon zest, and simmer, stirring occasionally, 30 minutes, or until the pumpkin is very soft.

Transfer the soup to a blender or food processor. Blend the mixture until you achieve your desired consistency: Blending the soup about 10 seconds creates a chunky pumpkin chowder, while blending longer creates a smooth purée.

Transfer the soup back to the pot and reheat over medium heat until slightly bubbly. Stir in the milk and simmer 1 minute. Remove the soup from the heat, season with lemon juice, and serve immediately.

*Yields 10 cups; serves 4-6*

# HARVEST PISTOU

### Pistou

3½ cups Genovese basil leaves

8 cloves garlic, peeled

¾ cup freshly grated
  Parmagiano-Reggiano
  cheese

½ cup olive oil

1 teaspoon salt

¼ teaspoon freshly ground
  black pepper

### Soup

12 cups rich chicken broth

2 cups dried cannellini beans,
  soaked and drained

¼ cup virgin olive oil

3 cups chopped new red
  potatoes

2 cups chopped hot white
  onions

1 cup chopped sweet yellow
  onions

2 cups chopped fresh carrots

2 cups of 1-inch pieces of fresh
  green beans

12 cups shredded cabbage

1 leek, sliced

1 cup chopped turnips

½ cup chopped pancetta or
  bacon

3 sage leaves

1 bay leaf

1 teaspoon salt

½ teaspoon freshly ground
  white pepper

*Pistou has been a favorite among the peoples of Italy and France for many years. You can enjoy this combination of basil, garlic, cheese, and olive oil with a variety of tomato sauces as well as soups. It's a favorite at my house when added to a stew of fresh vegetables. This recipe makes a big batch (16 cups) of pistou—one that utilizes a fair amount of fresh vegetables and herbs from the garden. However, you can easily halve the ingredients for a smaller pot of soup.*

*For the pistou,* in a blender or food processor, combine the basil, garlic, cheese, oil, salt, and pepper about 30 seconds, or until a smooth paste is formed. Transfer to a small bowl, cover, and set aside.

*For the soup,* in a large stockpot, bring the broth to a boil. Add the beans and parboil 45 minutes, then simmer over low heat while preparing the vegetables.

In a large frying pan or Dutch oven, heat the oil. Add the potatoes and onions, and sauté 5 minutes. Add the carrots, green beans, cabbage, leeks, and turnips. Stirring with a slotted spoon, sauté 10 minutes.

Transfer the vegetables to the pot of broth. Add the pancetta, sage, bay leaf, salt, and white pepper. Partially cover and simmer over medium-low heat 1 hour. The soup should be fairly thick and chunky. If you like less broth, allow the soup to cook longer.

When ready to serve, heat the soup over medium heat, then add the pistou, stirring it gently into the soup until blended. Transfer to warm crocks and serve immediately.

*Yields 4 quarts; serves 12-16*

*Note: The pistou stores well in the freezer up to 3 months, and the soup tastes best when prepared a day in advance.*

# FROG LEG STEW

2 tablespoons olive oil
2 tablespoons butter
1 cup chopped Frog's Leg
shallots
½ cup diced white globe
onions
⅓ cup chopped fresh celery
leaves
½ cup diced red bell peppers
½ cup diced celery
3 cups chopped, packed fresh
Swiss chard
½ cup tomato paste
4 cups bottled clam juice
2 bay leaves
½ cup chopped fresh flat-leaf
parsley
1 tablespoon chopped fresh
tarragon
½ teaspoon fresh lemon thyme
1 pound Alaskan cod, cut into
1-inch cubes
½ pound bay scallops
1 cup raw tubetti or tubettini
pasta
salt, to taste
½ teaspoon freshly ground
white pepper
⅛ teaspoon lemon zest

*S*hallots, not frogs, occupy center stage here. The French red shallot called Frog's Leg actually has the shape of that little creature's leg. Try this shallot with vegetables, herbs, and fish for a winter soup that takes the edge off the coldest of bones. If you can't get Frog's Legs, substitute another red shallot.

In a large stockpot, heat the oil and butter over medium heat until the butter melts. Add the shallots, onions, celery leaves, peppers, and celery, and sauté 10 minutes, or until the mixture begins to soften. Add the Swiss chard and cook 5 minutes.

Add the tomato paste, clam juice, and bay leaves, and bring to a boil. Reduce the heat to low, partially cover, and simmer 10 minutes. Add the parsley, tarragon, lemon thyme, cod, scallops, and pasta. Stir and cook over medium-low heat 10-15 minutes, or until the fish and pasta are cooked yet firm. Season with salt, stir in the white pepper and lemon zest, and simmer 1 minute. Transfer to warm bowls and serve immediately.

*Yields 8 cups*

*Note: This soup can be prepared 3-4 hours in advance of serving, then gently reheated.*

# Main Dishes

top: *Herb-Crusted Turkey*
*with Leek Stuffing*
*(recipe on page 120);*
*middle: Onion Rolls*
*(recipe on page 93);*
*bottom: Orange and Beet Salad*
*(recipe on page 78)*

# HERB-CRUSTED TURKEY
# WITH LEEK STUFFING

**Stuffing**

½ stick butter

1 cup chopped green garlic

4 heads garlic, chopped

1½ cups chopped leeks, white parts

two 24-ounce loaves white bread, cut into ½-inch cubes and dried in a deep glass pan 6-8 hours

1 cup chopped fresh parsley

¼ cup finely chopped fresh sage

1 teaspoon fine sea salt

1 tablespoon freshly ground white pepper

2 ounces pancetta, chopped

½ cup golden raisins

3-4 cups chicken or turkey broth

**Turkey and Herb Crust**

one 20-22-pound fresh turkey

2 tablespoons fresh thyme

1 tablespoon chopped fresh opal basil

1 cup minced fresh parsley

¼ cup chopped fresh tarragon

⅛ teaspoon dried ground ginger

1 teaspoon fine sea salt

1 teaspoon freshly ground white pepper

¼ cup olive oil

*S*pringtime supplies a compendium of young flavorful herbs, green garlic, and leeks (all tender and sweet) that combine to enhance roasted turkey. The result is a medley of peppery, cinnamon, clove, and lemon flavors that blend well with poultry. This combination goes well with a variety of vegetables, yet side dishes of baked apples, stuffed acorn squash, steamed spinach with chive butter, and freshly made applesauce appear before my guests again and again. This dish offers plenty of flavor without the heavy feeling that sometimes follows such a meal. A German Auslese wine makes a pleasant addition here. While this recipe does take a little time, the stuffing and the herb mix for the crust can be made a day in advance, leaving the actual turkey roast for the day of the dinner. (Photo on page 118.)

*For the stuffing,* in a large frying pan, melt the butter over medium heat. Sauté the garlic and leeks 20 minutes, or until translucent. Transfer to the pan that contains the bread, and toss until blended. Add the parsley, sage, salt, and white pepper, and blend into the stuffing mixture. Add the pancetta, raisins, and 3 cups of the broth. Add more broth if you want a moister stuffing. Cover and refrigerate until ready to use.

*For the turkey and herb crust,* remove any parts from the chest and neck cavity of the turkey. (You can reserve the parts for future use or discard them.) Rub the inside and outside of the turkey with salt, then rinse 5-7 minutes under cold water. Rest the turkey in a colander, and allow it to drain 15 minutes.

Preheat the oven to 325°F.

In a small bowl, whisk together the thyme, basil, parsley, tarragon, ginger, salt, white pepper, and oil. Set aside.

*To assemble*, place the turkey in a large bowl or on a flat work surface, then spoon the stuffing into the chest and neck cavities. Fill each cavity with plenty of stuffing, but do not pack tightly, as that would disallow moisture evaporation and result in soggy, sticky stuffing. Close the cavities with 4-inch to 5-inch skewers. Place the turkey on its back on a rack in a roasting pan.

Add 1 inch water to the bottom of the pan, and cover the turkey with a loose tent of foil. Roast the turkey 15-20 minutes per pound. During the last 30 minutes of roasting, spoon the herb mixture over the breast, wings, and legs. The turkey is completely cooked when a drumstick can be easily jiggled away from the body and the meat releases clear juice. Any pink juice indicates that the meat needs to cook a while longer. If you use a meat thermometer, it should register 180°F when inserted in the thickest meat of a thigh.

Remove the turkey from the oven, and allow it to rest 20 minutes. Since herbs darken easily in the oven, you may want to gently rub them away before carving.

*Serves 15-20*

*Note: This stuffing recipe deliberately calls for more ingredients than needed to stuff a 22-pound turkey. Use the 10 cups additional stuffing with the leftover turkey, or place it in airtight plastic containers and store unbaked in the freezer 6-8 weeks.*

# GARLIC-GINGER SALMON

one 2-pound red salmon fillet
or side
1 Vidalia onion, thinly sliced
2 tablespoons soy sauce
2 tablespoons sweet sherry
4 teaspoons minced fresh
ginger
juice of ½ lemon
2 yellow shallots, peeled and
chopped
1 clove elephant garlic,
chopped
¼ cup drained capers, rinsed,
garnish
¼ cup golden caviar, garnish

*W*hen red salmon is in season, grill it with garlic and ginger.
  *Serve this main dish with a salad of tossed greens laced with a
soy vinaigrette sauce and a dessert of sliced oranges, pears, and melon
to bring smiles from the guests at your table. The grilling sauce can be
made several hours in advance, making this a dinner that assembles
easily for an informal supper with friends.*

Place the salmon in a heatproof
dish and cover with the onions.
Set aside.

In a blender, place the soy sauce,
sherry, ginger, lemon juice, shallots,
and garlic. Whir at high speed
2-3 minutes, or until the ingredients
form a sauce. Pour the sauce over
the salmon, then grill over medium
heat 20-30 minutes, or until the
salmon is flaky. If desired, garnish
with the capers and caviar. Serve
immediately.

*Serves 4-6*

*Garlic-Ginger Salmon
(recipe this page)*

# PASTA *PUTTANESCA*

¼ cup olive oil

3½ cups seeded and diced
plum tomatoes, or one
28-ounce can diced plum
tomatoes

5 cloves garlic, minced

½ cup chopped red bell
peppers

½ teaspoon fine sea salt

¼ teaspoon ground red
pepper

4 flat anchovy fillets, rinsed
and diced

½ cup pitted kalamata olives

½ cup pitted green olives

1 tablespoon salt

1 pound fresh egg linguine

½ cup chopped fresh green
Genovese basil

1 tablespoon grated Pecorino
Romano cheese, garnish

*P*uttanesca *sauce derives its name from "puttana," which is Italian for streetwalker or prostitute. Many believe the sauce was so named because the ingredients are not only seductive but entrancing enough to keep you coming back for more. It has also been said that prostitutes made this sauce to get and keep customers at their doors. At any rate, this pasta sauce is definitely worth a try, or two, or three.... (Photo on page 102.)*

In a large frying pan, heat the oil over low heat. Sauté the tomatoes 5 minutes, then add the garlic and peppers and simmer another 5 minutes. Add the salt, red pepper, anchovies, and olives. Stir and simmer 10 minutes. Lower the heat to keep the sauce warm.

In a large pot, bring 3 quarts water with the salt to a boil. Add the pasta and cook 5-7 minutes, or until tender. Drain in a colander.

Place the pasta in a large bowl, add the sauce, and toss. Toss in the basil, and garnish with the cheese. Serve immediately.

*Yields 2 cups sauce; serves 3-4*

# FARFALLE WITH ROASTED SHALLOT SAUCE

1¼ cups Sauternes or other
   dry white wine
15 cloves garlic, roasted,
   peeled, and coarsely
   mashed
8 yellow shallots, roasted,
   peeled, and coarsely
   mashed
2 tablespoons chopped
   Preserved Lemons (see
   page 155)
2¼ cups heavy cream
¼ teaspoon salt
¼ teaspoon freshly ground
   white pepper
1 pound farfalle or bow-tie
   pasta
½ cup chopped fresh opal basil
¼ cup toasted hazelnuts,
   hulled and halved, garnish

*Oven-roasted shallots combine with the tang of preserved lemons and the body of heavy cream to create a truly wonderful sauce for farfalle pasta. The sauce could also be used to festoon cheese tortelloni for a heartier table masterpiece. Not much is needed here to create a meal, beyond a salad of tossed greens and a plate of oranges and sliced table cheese. The sauce can be made a day in advance and can be doubled easily, allowing you to add a guest or two for dinner.*

In a medium saucepan, heat the wine over medium heat 5 minutes. Add the garlic, shallots, and lemons. Bring the mixture to a boil, then reduce the heat to medium, cover, and simmer 20 minutes. Add the heavy cream, salt, and white pepper, and simmer, uncovered, over low heat 25 minutes, or until the liquid is slightly reduced. If desired, season with more salt and pepper. Cover and keep warm.

Bring 4 quarts salted water to a boil, then add the pasta and cook over medium heat 12-15 minutes, or until the pasta is chewy, or *al dente*. Drain the pasta, and transfer to a warm serving bowl. Add the sauce and basil, and toss to coat the pasta. Garnish with hazelnuts. Serve immediately.

*Yields 2¾ cups sauce; serves 4-6*

# CHICKEN AND SHRIMP GRILLED WITH LEMON-GARLIC SALSA

## Salsa
1½ cups olive oil
½ cup chopped Preserved
Lemons (see page 155)
½ cup chopped red onions
2 cloves garlic, peeled and
chopped
1 jalapeño chile, finely
chopped
2 cups seeded, chopped fresh
plum tomatoes
1 teaspoon salt
½ teaspoon freshly ground
black pepper
1 tablespoon chopped fresh
parsley

## Chicken and Shrimp
4 boneless, skinless chicken
breasts, halved
8 jumbo shrimp, cleaned,
deveined, and butterflied
½ cup virgin olive oil
½ tablespoon fresh lemon juice
½ tablespoon fresh lime juice
6 cloves garlic, peeled and
finely chopped
1 tablespoon chopped fresh
tarragon

*T*he salsa for this dish can be made several days in advance and warmed up when ready to grill. This recipe doubles and even triples easily, making it a delicious yet simple way to serve 8-12 guests. This dish is wonderful with fresh corn and sliced tomatoes.

*For the salsa*, heat the oil over medium heat in a small saucepan. Sauté the lemons, onions, garlic, and chiles 5-10 minutes minutes, or until the onions and garlic are soft. Add the tomatoes, salt, and pepper, and simmer another 10 minutes. Remove the pan from the heat, then stir in the parsley and set aside or refrigerate until ready to use.

*For the chicken and shrimp*, place the chicken and shrimp in a single layer in a shallow baking dish and set aside.

In a small saucepan, heat the oil, lemon juice, lime juice, garlic, and tarragon over low heat 5 minutes. Remove the pan from the heat, and set aside 10 minutes to cool.

Pour the marinade over the chicken and shrimp, coating all pieces. Cover the dish and refrigerate at least 8 hours, turning the chicken and shrimp once.

When ready to grill, remove the salsa from the refrigerator and allow it to reach room temperature. Place the chicken on the grill over medium-hot heat. Grill 10-12 minutes, turning after 5-7 minutes. Place the shrimp on the grill and cook 5-10 minutes, or until the shrimp turn bright pink and are cooked through.

Transfer the chicken and shrimp to a warm serving dish and top with the salsa. Serve immediately, with additional salsa on the side.

*Serves 4*

*Note: The salsa can be preserved in half-pint jars, where it remains tasty up to 6 months.*

# GRILLED SALMON
# WITH GREEN GARLIC MAYONNAISE

one 2-pound salmon fillet
   or side
¼ cup fresh lime juice
¼ teaspoon freshly ground
   white pepper
2 tablespoons soy sauce
Green Garlic Mayonnaise,
   1 recipe (see page 152)
1 hard-boiled egg, sliced,
   garnish
½ cup green cerignola olives,
   garnish

*G*reen Garlic Mayonnaise enhances salmon for a light yet aromatic luncheon or dinner course. The combination of tangy mayonnaise, green olives, and mellow egg slices is easy to assemble and serve. The marinade can be made a day in advance, so this is a meal that's perfect for cooking and visiting with guests simultaneously. (Photo on page 150.)

Place the salmon in a heatproof dish and set aside.

In a small bowl, whisk together the lime juice, white pepper, and soy sauce. Brush the mixture onto the salmon. Allow the salmon to marinate 15 minutes, then grill over medium heat 10-15 minutes, or until the salmon is flaky. Top with the Green Garlic Mayonnaise, and garnish with the eggs and olives. Serve immediately or serve at room temperature.

*Serves 4-6*

# DEEP-DISH SPANISH ONIONS

¼ cup olive oil
1 cup chopped yellow Spanish
    onions
1 cup chopped red Spanish
    onions
3 Cubanelle or other thin-
    skinned Italian frying pep-
    pers, seeded and chopped
2 orange bell peppers, seeded
    and chopped
1 yellow bell pepper, seeded
    and chopped
1 jalapeño chile, seeded and
    chopped
4 large cloves rocambole
    garlic, chopped
1 teaspoon salt
1 tablespoon chopped fresh
    *epazote*
½ teaspoon ground dried
    ancho chile
1 teaspoon ground cumin
1 teaspoon lime juice
3 tablespoons flour
4 eggs
1 cup heavy cream
½ cup buttermilk
8 ounces sharp white Cheddar
    cheese, shredded
½ cup chopped fresh cilantro,
    optional

*T*he combination of onions, peppers, and herbs is one that I use more than others. The blend in this recipe of Spanish onions, Cubanelles, garlic, and red bells supplies a satisfying side dish that is savory and not too heavy. It also makes a good luncheon dish. Just add salad and bread for a nutritious and warming meal.

Preheat the oven to 375°F.

In a large frying pan, heat the oil over medium heat. Sauté the onions, peppers, and jalapeño chiles 15 minutes. Add the garlic, salt, *epazote*, ancho chile, cumin, and lime juice, and sauté 10-12 minutes, or until there is no excess liquid. Remove the pan from the heat, then blend in the flour with a slotted spoon.

In a medium bowl, whisk together the eggs, heavy cream, and buttermilk.

Add one-half of the cheese to the onion-pepper mixture, blending thoroughly. Spoon the mixture into a greased, ovenproof 2-quart casserole or soufflé dish. Pour the egg mixture over the vegetables, making sure that the liquid is evenly distributed. Top with the remaining cheese, and bake 35-40 minutes.

Allow the dish to set 5 minutes before serving. If desired, top with cilantro. Serve immediately.

*Serves 4-6*

# PENNE WITH GARLIC AND WILD MIXED MUSHROOMS

1 pound fresh cremini mushrooms

1 pound fresh white mushrooms

½ pound fresh oyster or shiitake mushrooms

½ cup olive oil

½ cup chopped white onions

¼ cup chopped garlic

1 tablespoon dry Marsala wine

2 pounds penne pasta

½ cup heavy cream

½ cup half-and-half

3 tablespoons sweet, unsalted butter

½ teaspoon freshly ground black pepper

¼ cup chopped fresh flat-leaf parsley

1 tablespoon chopped fresh oregano

1 cup shredded Parmagiano-Reggiano cheese

*P*enne was originally derived from small squares of dough with points at either end. Cooks called the shape "penne," which translates to "quill" in Italian. The makers of this pasta achieved the shape by taking opposite points of the dough and pressing them together around a dowel. The dowels they used were ribbed, thus creating grooves in the quills. Today, many commercial brands of penne are smooth, but if you are ambitious enough to make your own, you can achieve the original ribbed quill by using a pencil and a comb.

Rinse, drain, and cut the mushrooms into thin slices. (You may want to cut the stems, which can be fibrous, from the oyster or shiitake mushrooms and set aside for another use before cutting the caps into thin slices.)

In a large, heavy, nonstick pot, heat the oil over medium heat. Sauté the onions and garlic 8 minutes. Add the wine and mushrooms, stirring with a slotted spoon. Simmer over medium-low heat 15-20 minutes, or until the liquid is cooked out of the mushrooms. Set aside.

In a large stockpot, bring 6 quarts water and 2 tablespoons salt to a boil over high heat. Add the pasta and cook 15-20 minutes, stirring occasionally to prevent the pasta from sticking.

While the pasta is cooking, return the mushroom mixture to the stove over low heat. Stir in the heavy cream, half-and-half, butter, and pepper. Increase the heat to medium-high, and stir continuously until the liquid is reduced by half and the mixture is creamy. Stir in the parsley and oregano, then reduce the heat to warm.

Drain the pasta and transfer to a warm, deep serving platter or shallow bowl. Add the mushroom mixture, and toss to blend the ingredients. Add the cheese, toss again, and serve.

*Serves 8-10*

# LAMB SHANKS, GARLIC, AND MINT

4 fresh lamb shanks
2 large heads garlic, roasted,
  peeled, and mashed
2 large cloves elephant garlic,
  minced
2 tablespoons fresh lemon
  juice
1 teaspoon freshly ground
  white pepper
1 teaspoon salt
⅓ cup virgin olive oil
⅝ cup chopped fresh mint

*Garlic, mint, and lemon add tang and levity to the somewhat complex flavor of lamb. This main dish serves well with basil couscous and a salad of greens tossed with mandarin oranges. The garlic sauce can be prepared a day in advance and warmed to room temperature when ready to use.*

Preheat the oven to 375°F. Place the lamb in an ovenproof baking dish and set aside.

In a small bowl, blend the garlic, lemon juice, white pepper, salt, and oil with a fork until a chunky paste is formed. Stir in the mint, then spoon-paste on all sides of the lamb.

Add ½ inch water to the bottom of the baking dish. Roast the lamb 1-1¼ hours, or until the lamb is tender, brown, and cooked through. Transfer the lamb to a serving platter, and let stand 5-7 minutes before serving.

*Serves 4-6*

*Lamb Shanks, Garlic, and Mint*
*(recipe this page)*

# MOUSSAKA

1½ pounds eggplant
7-8 tablespoons olive oil
1½ pounds loose ground lamb
¾ cup chopped sweet onions
2 cloves garlic, chopped
6 ounces canned tomato paste
½ cup water
⅛ teaspoon cinnamon
Moussaka Cheese Sauce,
    1 recipe, or ¼ cup grated
    Parmesan or Greek kasseri
    cheese

**Moussaka Cheese Sauce**
1 cup small-curd cottage
    cheese, drained
½ cup grated Parmesan cheese
⅛ teaspoon freshly ground
    white pepper
3 tablespoons sweet, unsalted
    butter
3 tablespoons flour
¼ teaspoon ground nutmeg
½ cup heavy cream
¼ cup beef bouillon or canned
    broth
1 egg, beaten

*M*ake a batch of moussaka and take advantage of the bounty of eggplant and onions available at harvesttime. Moussaka is Greek in origin and traditionally served with the cheese sauce included here. Enjoy this dish with a chilled retsina wine and fresh fruit for dessert.

Peel the eggplant and cut into ¼-inch-thick slices. Place the eggplant in a large bowl containing 2 quarts water and 1 tablespoon salt, and top the bowl with a plate to keep the eggplant immersed. Soak the eggplant 30 minutes, then drain and set aside on a baking sheet lined with paper towels to dry.

In a large, nonstick frying pan, heat 2 tablespoons of the oil over medium heat. Brown the lamb 10 minutes. Using a slotted spoon, transfer to a medium bowl and set aside.

Preheat the oven broiler.

Place another 2 tablespoons of the oil in the frying pan, add the onions and garlic, and sauté over medium heat 5 minutes. Add the tomato paste, water, and cinnamon, stirring with a wooden spoon until the ingredients are blended. Simmer 10 minutes over medium-low heat, then stir in the lamb. Remove from the heat and set aside.

Place a single layer of eggplant on a baking sheet and brush with 2 tablespoons of the oil. Broil

5-7 minutes, or until golden. Turn the slices over, brush with the remaining oil, and broil another 5-7 minutes, or until golden. Remove the eggplant from the oven, then lower the heat to 350°F.

In a greased, 2-quart ovenproof casserole or deep baking dish, layer one-half of the eggplant, then one-half of the meat mixture. Repeat, and top with the Moussaka Cheese Sauce or cheese. Bake 40-45 minutes. Allow the moussaka to stand, uncovered, 10 minutes before serving.

*Serves 4-6*

**Moussaka Cheese Sauce**

Combine the cheeses and pepper in a blender or food processor until smooth. Refrigerate until ready to use.

In a medium saucepan, melt the butter over medium heat. Add the flour and nutmeg, and stir until the mixture begins to bubble. Add the heavy cream and bouillon, and simmer, stirring constantly, over low heat until the sauce begins to thicken. Remove the pan from the heat, then whisk in the egg until the ingredients are blended.

Return the sauce to the low heat, then stir in the cheese mixture with a whisk until smooth and blended. Simmer 2 minutes and remove from the heat.

# LEEK AND CHICKEN POTPIE

**Crust**
1 egg
⅓ cup whole milk
2½ cups sifted flour
1 teaspoon salt
3 tablespoons shortening

**Potpie**
2 red-skinned sweet potatoes
½ cup water
2 stalks celery, chopped
2 carrots, chopped
2 cups chopped leeks, white
 parts
1 cup diced fresh fennel
4 heads garlic, roasted,
 peeled, and mashed
3 heaping tablespoons flour
1 teaspoon fine sea salt
1 teaspoon freshly ground
 white pepper
one 3-pound chicken, steeped,
 skinned, and shredded, or
 4 cups of ¾-inch cubed
 chicken
3 cups chicken broth
2 tablespoons chopped fresh
 lemon thyme
¼ cup minced fresh chives

*U*nlike some recipes for potpie, this recipe doesn't offer crust on the sides or as dividing layers within the "pot." This recipe comes together in a cast-iron skillet with the crust adorning the top only. While it takes a little time to assemble everything, the result is worth the work and the wait. The potpie mixture can be placed in airtight containers (without the crust, of course) and saved for up to 3 months in the freezer. The crust can be made a day in advance and refrigerated until ready to use.

*For the crust*, in a small bowl, whisk the egg until creamy and lemon-colored. Stir in the milk. In a medium bowl, blend the flour and salt with a fork, then blend in the shortening. Add the egg mixture and blend thoroughly, making a soft, pliable dough. If the dough feels a bit stiff, add a little more milk. Cover with plastic wrap and refrigerate until ready to use.

*For the potpie*, preheat the oven to 375°F. Wrap the sweet potatoes in foil and bake 1 hour. Set aside to cool.

In a 10-inch or 12-inch cast-iron skillet, heat the water over medium heat. Cook the celery, carrots, leeks, and fennel 15 minutes. Add the garlic, flour, salt, white pepper, and chicken, stirring with a large spoon until the flour is blended throughout the mixture. Add the broth and simmer over low heat.

Peel and cut the sweet potatoes into ½-inch cubes, then add to the chicken mixture. Add the lemon thyme and chives.

Preheat the oven to 375°F again.

*To assemble*, roll out the dough on a lightly floured surface until it is ¼ inch thick. Using a biscuit or cookie cutter, cut the dough into shapes, then place the shapes on top of the potpie about ¼ in. apart. Bake 35-45 minutes, or until the crust is golden and the pie begins to bubble. Allow the potpie to cool 10-15 minutes before serving.

*Serves 8-10*

*Leek and Chicken Potpie
(recipe this page)*

# STEAK AND ONION PIE

**Dough**
4-4½ cups sifted bread flour
1½ teaspoons salt
½ cup vegetable shortening
4 large eggs, beaten
¾ cup light cream or half-and-half
½ cup sweet, unsalted butter, chipped

**Filling**
¼ cup vegetable oil
1½ pounds boneless chuck, cut into 1-inch cubes
½ pound fresh lamb, cut into 1-inch cubes
½ cup chopped white winter onions
½ cup chopped sweet red onions
¼ cup flour
½ cup canned beef broth
½ cup Burgundy wine
1 teaspoon salt
1 teaspoon freshly ground black pepper
¼ teaspoon ground red pepper
1 teaspoon Worcestershire sauce
1 teaspoon Dijon mustard

*M*y favorite recipe for steak and kidney pie inspired the adaptation offered here. While both are delicious, the ingredients for Steak and Onion Pie are more accessible. It's also a lighter dish for those who prefer the coziness of potpie without the sometimes serious flavor that kidneys provide.

*For the dough,* blend 4 cups of the flour with ½ teaspoon of the salt and the shortening in a large bowl. In a small bowl, mix the eggs with the light cream. Add all but 2 tablespoons of the egg mixture to the flour mixture, and knead until smooth. Cover and refrigerate the remaining egg mixture to be used as a glaze before baking.

Roll the dough into a rectangle about ⅛ inch thick, and dot with bits of one-half of the butter. Sift a little flour over the butter, then fold the long ends of the dough toward the center. Fold the long ends of the dough toward the center a second time, then roll into a ⅛-inch-thick sheet. Dot the dough with the remaining butter and fold as before. Place the dough in a small bowl, cover with plastic, and refrigerate.

*For the filling,* in a large frying pan or Dutch oven, heat the oil over medium heat. Brown the chuck and lamb in batches until all sides are brown. Transfer to a large plate and set aside.

Place the onions in the pan and sauté 10 minutes. Return the meat to the pan, then dust the meat and onions with the flour until well coated. Cook 2-3 minutes, stirring once. Stir in the broth and wine, and bring the mixture to a low boil over medium-high heat. Add the salt, black pepper, red pepper, Worcestershire, and mustard, and blend well.

Partially cover the mixture and simmer over low heat 1½ hours, or until the meat is tender. The meat should be nearly covered with liquid as it cooks, so add a little more broth or water, if necessary. Lower the heat to warm.

Preheat the oven to 425°F.

*To assemble*, roll out the dough to a thickness of ⅛ inch. Cut a circle about 1 inch wider than the top of a deep pie dish or casserole that will be used to cover the pie. Use the remaining scraps of dough to line the sides and bottom of the dish.

Spoon the filling into the dish. Cover with the dough circle, and press the dough to the rim of the dish. Brush the top of the pie with the reserved egg mixture, then pierce the top 3-4 times with a knife.

Place the pie on a baking sheet and bake 10 minutes. Reduce the heat to 350°F and bake another 15-20 minutes, or until the pie is bubbly and the crust is golden. Allow the pie to rest 10 minutes. Slice into wedges or squares and serve.

*Serves 6*

*Note: This recipe is also attractive in a square or oblong casserole with a lattice top crust. This dish doubles easily and keeps well in the freezer up to 6 months.*

# TAGLIATELLE AL TONNO

2 tablespoons butter
2 tablespoons olive oil
6 fresh cremini mushrooms,
 thinly sliced
¼ cup chopped sweet onions
¼ cup chopped elephant garlic
2 tablespoons snipped garlic
 chives
1 cup rich chicken broth
½ cup Sauternes or vermouth
½ teaspoon salt
½ teaspoon freshly ground
 white pepper
16 ounces fresh tuna, cut into
 1-inch cubes
1 pound tagliatelle pasta
⅓ cup heavy cream
1 tablespoon drained capers,
 rinsed
¼-⅓ cup chopped fresh
 Genovese basil

*The seas surrounding the Italian islands of Sicily and Sardinia offer a bounty of delicious fish. Islanders have cast their nets into the ocean for centuries, resulting in a yield of squid, eel, tuna, and delicacies not readily available from American shores. This recipe for tagliatelle with tuna is a traditional dish that pays respect to the fine flavor of its Mediterranean cousin.*

In a large frying pan, heat the butter and oil over medium heat. Sauté the mushrooms, onions, garlic, and chives 5 minutes. Add the broth, Sauternes, salt, and white pepper, and simmer 15 minutes. Add the tuna, and gently toss until all of the ingredients are blended. Cook another 5-7 minutes, or until the tuna is firm and barely cooked through. Lower the heat to warm and cover while cooking the pasta.

In a medium stockpot, bring 2 quarts water and 1 tablespoon salt to a boil. Cook the pasta, stirring occasionally, 10-15 minutes, or until the pasta is *al dente*. Just before the pasta is done, increase the heat to medium-low under the tuna mixture, and blend in the heavy cream and capers.

Drain the pasta and transfer to a warm bowl. Toss in the tuna mixture and basil. Serve immediately.

*Serves 4*

*Note: This recipe doubles easily.*

# ONION HARVEST PIE

2 pounds fresh green Swiss
   chard, stems and leaves
   chopped separately
2 eggs
1 cup ricotta cheese
¼ cup freshly grated
   Parmagiano-Reggiano
   cheese
¼ teaspoon ground nutmeg
¼ teaspoon fine sea salt
¼ teaspoon finely ground
   black pepper
½ cup minced pancetta
1 large white winter onion,
   diced
3 cloves rocambole or regular
   garlic, minced
¼ cup golden seedless raisins
2 unbaked pastry sheets,
   thawed

*Although this harvest pie calls for pancetta, the primary ingredients of Swiss chard, onions, raisins, and spices offer a flavorful and healthy vegetarian alternate. This is based on a recipe for Italian spinach pie, which has been traced back to the Tuscan tables of the 15th century. You may want to try the recipe with Swiss chard during the summer, then with spinach and your stored onions during the winter.*

In a large pot, bring ¼ cup water to a boil. Cook the Swiss chard stems 5 minutes, then add the Swiss chard leaves, cover, and cook 5 minutes, or until the greens are bright with color yet pliable. Drain the Swiss chard and set aside.

In a medium bowl, whisk the eggs. Stir in the cheeses, nutmeg, salt, and pepper, and set aside.

In a 12-inch frying pan, sauté the pancetta over low heat 5-7 minutes. Add the onions and garlic, and cook another 5 minutes. Add the Swiss chard and raisins, and blend well. Remove the pan from the heat, then add the cheese mixture, blending all the ingredients with a spoon.

Preheat the oven to 350°F.

Grease a 9-inch or 10-inch springform pan with butter. Roll out one pastry sheet to a thickness of ⅛ inch to ¼ inch. Line the bottom and sides of the pan with the sheet. Spoon the Swiss chard mixture into the pan. Roll the second pastry sheet into a 10-inch circle, and cover the top of the pan. Press the edges of the pastry together all the way around the pie, fluting slightly if desired.

Place the pie on a baking sheet, and bake 40-45 minutes, or until the top is flaky and golden. Remove the sides from the pan. Allow the pie to rest 10 minutes before cutting. Serve hot.

*Serves 8-10*

*Note: Pancetta is available in a number of Italian groceries and delicatessens. If you can't find it, you can substitute a good-quality cured bacon.*

# BASIL-RED CURRY COD

4 dried pasilla chiles
4 dried mirasol chiles
4 dried Thai chiles
1 teaspoon ground coriander
   seeds
½ teaspoon freshly ground
   white pepper
½ teaspoon ground cumin
½ teaspoon nutmeg
1 teaspoon fine sea salt
1 tablespoon fresh lime zest
1 tablespoon dried cilantro
1 tablespoon chopped fresh
   ginger
5 cloves garlic, chopped
two 10-ounce cans coconut
   milk
1½ pounds Alaskan cod fillet
1 teaspoon paprika, garnish
1 cup fresh Genovese basil
   leaves, garnish

*A*sian recipes, particularly those from Thailand, contain a seemingly unlikely combination of sweet and hot ingredients. This recipe for red curry cod combines a blend of chiles with coconut milk and fresh green basil. You'll have enough curry sauce for the fish and extra for the freezer, where it keeps well up to 3 months. If you don't want extra sauce, simply halve the recipe. Red curry also complements poultry, rice, and noodle dishes with flavor as well as nutrition.

Soak the pasilla and mirasol chiles in 2 cups water 20 minutes, or until they are pliable and somewhat soft. Remove the stems and seeds and discard.

Preheat the oven to 375°F.

Place the chiles, coriander, white pepper, cumin, nutmeg, salt, lime zest, cilantro, ginger, and garlic in a blender. Add 1 can of the coconut milk and mix at high speed 30 seconds. Add the remaining coconut milk and blend 1 minute. Remove and discard the Thai chiles.

Place the cod in an ovenproof baking dish. Pour 1¼ cups of the sauce over the cod, and bake 35-45 minutes. Garnish with the paprika and basil. Serve immediately.

*Serves 4-6*

*Basil-Red Curry Cod*
*(recipe this page)*

# HOMEMADE SAUSAGE

The age-old process of making sausage began in Europe and thrives to the present day. Most Western and Eastern countries produce an array of sausages for daily consumption. Be they mild, hot, pork, veal, beef, or lamb, sausages frequently come seasoned with crushed red pepper, fennel, rosemary, garlic, pine nuts, or grated Romano cheese. Portuguese linguisa, German bratwurst, and Polish keilbasa are just a few examples of how cooks from various countries try their hands at uniting meats, spices, and casings.

In recent years, Americans have explored recipes that go beyond traditional meats and seasonings. Apples, chicken, turkey, and a variety of culinary herbs, from basil and parsley to lemon verbena and lemon thyme, have expanded our appreciation of sausage in restaurants and in the kitchen. Making homemade sausage is a fairly simple and satisfying process. And it's a treat to find yourself doing something that you thought only the butcher could do. Here are a few guidelines for creating a bounty of sausage that can be eaten fresh or put in the freezer for future use.

• If you don't have a sausage maker, use a heavy-duty mixer with a meat-grinding attachment to produce perfect ground sausage in minutes. You can also coarsely chop meat with a sharp cleaver or a heavy-duty food processor.

• While many butchers are happy to stuff the sausage into casings, use the sausage-stuffing attachment for your mixer or sausage maker to perform this process at home. Try making sausage patties as well as a few links. Since links and patties cook up a little differently, you may enjoy exploring the flavor possibilities that come with each process.

• Look for animal casings (preferably pork) that are heavily salted because they will keep in the freezer several months. When you're ready to use the casings, allow them to defrost, then rinse thoroughly to remove excess salt or any bits of matter within the walls of the casing.

• Make sure that your equipment is clean and very cold. The ground sausage mixture should also be well chilled.

• When ready to stuff the casings, cut off the length that you'll need (3 feet typically accommodates 3 pounds of sausage meat), then soak the casing in cold water at least 30 minutes. Attach a casing end to the sink faucet and rinse with the coldest tap water about 10 minutes to thoroughly clean the insides. Tie a knot at one open end.

• Send 3 ounces to 4 ounces of sausage through the machine and into a bowl to dispense any air in the stuffing tube.

• Rinse the outside of the casing and the stuffing tube with cold water. Put the open end of the casing around the spout of the stuffing tube. Next, push the remaining casing onto the stuffing tube until all but 3 inches to 4 inches of the knotted end of the casing have been pushed onto the spout. Work as quickly as possible while the machinery and ingredients are chilled.

• Hold the casing end parallel to the stuffing tube and send the sausage meat through the machine. Once the casing is nearly filled, slip the open end off of the tube. Using a separate length of rinsed and chilled casing or strong kitchen string, tie 2 side-by-side knots in the casing at 5-inch intervals. Snip the links apart in between the knots with sharp kitchen shears.

• If you opt to make sausage patties, flatten the meat into circles that are 4 inches in diameter and ¼ inch to ⅜ inch thick.

• Freeze the sausage in airtight containers, or use right away on the grill or in the skillet.

# SPICY ITALIAN SAUSAGE

8 pounds lean Boston boneless
  shoulder pork, cut into
  1-inch cubes
⅓ cup salt
1 tablespoon coarsely ground
  black pepper
1 tablespoon red pepper flakes
¼ cup crushed garlic
1 tablespoon fennel seed
½ cup chopped fresh parsley

*This is a zesty recipe that freezes well for months and stays fresh 2-3 days in the refrigerator. This sausage is especially flavorful when grilled with a combination of hot and sweet Italian peppers, mushrooms, and yellow onions. If you'd like a sausage sandwich, use the pizza dough recipe (see page 95) and bake it into a baguette-style loaf. Whether you bake the bread or buy it, line it with thin slices of Asiago cheese before crowning it with the sausage and peppers.*

Pass the pork through a meat grinder or the sausage attachment to a mixer, using a blade with medium holes. Transfer to a marble work surface or a large, shallow bowl. Sprinkle the salt, black pepper, red pepper, garlic, fennel seed, and parsley over the pork. Gently mix in the seasonings with a fork or with your hands, being careful not to overwork or mash the sausage. Transfer to a smaller bowl or plastic bag, cover, and refrigerate 8 hours or overnight.

Remove about 2 tablespoons of the sausage from the refrigerator and form it into a small medallion.

In a small frying pan, cook 5-7 minutes on each side over medium heat. Taste and adjust the seasonings, if necessary. Correct the seasonings in the uncooked sausage, if desired. Form the sausage into patties or links. Use fresh or freeze for future use.

*Yields 24-32 patties or 6-10 links*

*Note: This sausage is good fresh for sandwiches or in pasta sauce. This recipe is also excellent on the grill.*

# LAMB SAUSAGE
# WITH HERBS AND GARLIC

3 pounds boneless lamb, cut
    into 1-inch cubes

¼ cup chopped fresh mint
    leaves

2 tablespoons chopped fresh
    rosemary

5 cloves garlic, mashed

½ cup Chianti or dry red wine

1½ teaspoons freshly ground
    black pepper

1 teaspoon salt

*I like to make this sausage into patties for the freezer, but you can also serve it fresh. It is particularly good in Greek Moussaka (see page 132). This recipe doubles easily.*

Pass the lamb through a meat grinder or the sausage attachment to a mixer, using a blade with large holes to make a slightly chunky sausage. For a finer sausage, pass the lamb through the grinder a second time. Transfer the lamb to a medium bowl.

In a small bowl, combine the mint, rosemary, garlic, wine, pepper, and salt until blended. Add to the lamb, and blend thoroughly with your hands or a fork. Cover the sausage and refrigerate 8 hours or overnight.

Remove about 2 tablespoons of the sausage from the refrigerator and form it into a small medallion. In a small frying pan, cook 5-7 minutes on each side over medium heat. Taste and adjust the seasonings, if necessary. Correct the seasonings in the uncooked sausage, if desired. Form the sausage into patties or links. Use fresh or freeze for future use.

*Yields six 8-inch patties or 5-6 links*

# SAUERBRATEN

one 3½-pound bottom rump
    roast
1 tablespoon salt
1 teaspoon freshly ground
    black pepper
2 cups red wine vinegar
1 cup red wine
2 mildly hot white onions,
    sliced
1 medium carrot, sliced
5 whole cloves
3 bay leaves
3 tablespoons sugar
3 green peppercorns, freshly
    ground
12-15 gingersnaps, crushed

*Sauerbraten and red cabbage assist in birthday celebrations at my house. Since Oktoberfest and my husband's birthday occur at about the same time of year, we enjoy a variety of foods from Hamburg and Bavaria once September closes its doors. This recipe complements boiled whole potatoes or potato dumplings. It is easy to serve to a large group for dinner, since the meat marinates for several days before cooking.*

Season all sides of the roast with the salt and black pepper, then place it in a deep bowl. Add the vinegar, wine, onions, carrots, cloves, and bay leaves. Turn the roast in the bowl so that the vegetables and liquids are on all sides of it. Cover with plastic wrap and marinate in the refrigerator 4 days.

On the fifth day, place the roast, vegetables, and marinade in a Dutch oven or large stockpot. Bring the mixture to a boil over medium-high heat, then reduce the heat to medium-low, partially cover, and simmer 2 hours.

In a small bowl, combine the sugar, green pepper, and ginger-snaps, and set aside.

Preheat the oven to "warm" or the lowest setting.

Remove the roast from the stock-pot, and place it in an ovenproof dish. Cover lightly with foil, then place the roast in the oven while preparing the gravy.

Remove the bay leaf and any large pieces of vegetables from the stockpot and discard. Whisk in the gingersnap mixture a little at a time, until a smooth, rich brown gravy is formed. Reduce the heat to low.

Remove the roast from the oven and cut into ¼-inch-thick slices. Ladle some of the gravy over the roast, and serve immediately. Serve additional gravy on the side.

*Serves 6-8*

# RAUCOUS ROAST DUCK

**Duck**
one 4-pound duck
½ teaspoon salt
1 orange, quartered
1 lime, quartered
6 large cloves garlic

**Sauce**
¾ cup orange juice
2 tablespoons lime juice
¼ cup soy sauce
½ cup chopped scallions,
  green and white parts
1 clove elephant garlic, minced
1 teaspoon freshly ground
  ginger

*D*uck is fair game for the grill, the oven, elegant dinners, and out-door country picnics. For centuries, cooks have graced this bird with berries, cherries, sauces, olives, figs, peppercorns, sweet potatoes, and more. Still, a delicious duck is simply dressed. It must be well drained of its fat, roasted slowly, and seasoned with tang and piquancy. By doing this, the duck will be tender, moist, and full of flavor, not drowned in a sea of sauces and sugars.

*For the duck,* sprinkle the outside of the duck with the salt, then place the oranges, limes, and garlic into the body cavity.

Pierce the skin of the duck with the tip of a paring knife, and place the duck breast side down on a poultry rack. Place in a shallow baking dish and set aside.

Preheat the oven to 375°F.

*For the sauce,* in a small saucepan, combine the juices, soy sauce, scallions, garlic, and ginger. Bring to a boil over medium heat, then reduce the heat and simmer 1 minute.

Lightly brush the duck with some of the sauce, and pour ½ inch water into the baking dish. Roast the duck 2¼ hours, basting every 20 minutes until all of the sauce is used. If necessary, add more water to the bottom of the dish to keep the level at ½ inch or the duck will be dry. Allow the duck to rest on the rack 10 minutes before carving.

*Serves 4*

*Raucous Roast Duck*
*(recipe this page)*

# TERIYAKI BEEF
# WITH TOASTED SESAME SEEDS

**Sauce**

2 cups wheat-free tamari sauce

1½ lemons, sliced

3 cloves rocambole or other
    strong garlic, sliced

1¼ cups cold water

1½ cups sugar

½ cup mirin wine

1 teaspoon grated fresh ginger

¼ cup cornstarch

**Roast**

one 3½-pound boneless chuck
    roast

1 medium red onion, chopped

2 medium Vidalia onions,
    chopped

2 cloves elephant garlic, cut
    lengthwise into ¼-inch slices

½ cup chopped scallions,
    green and white parts

¼ cup toasted sesame seeds,
    garnish

*S*ome years ago, a restaurant called Kobe An introduced Japanese cuisine as well as culture to many of us living in Boulder, Colorado. It was there that I began to understand the nutritional value of nori (dried seaweed), appreciate the flavors unique to dashi (soup stock), and learn the purposes for daikon (white radish) and wasabi (green horseradish).

From Kobe An came the inspiration for the teriyaki sauce used in this recipe. Although the restaurant no longer exists, its legacy has lived in my kitchen for more than a decade.

Preheat the oven to 375°F.

*For the sauce*, place the tamari sauce, lemons, garlic, 1 cup of the water, sugar, mirin, and ginger in a medium saucepan. Cook over medium heat until thoroughly heated.

In a small bowl, combine the cornstarch and the remaining water until well blended. Add to the sauce a little at a time, and cook 5-7 minutes, or until the sauce is smooth, dark, and thickened. Remove the pan from the heat and set aside.

*For the roast*, place the roast in an ovenproof baking dish that is about 3 inches to 4 inches deep. Brush all sides of the roast with some of the sauce, pour ¼ inch water into the dish, and bake, uncovered, 15 minutes. Baste the roast again on all sides with more of the sauce, cover loosely with a tent of foil, and reduce the temperature to 350°F.

Add the onions, garlic, and scallions, and cook 1¼ hours. If necessary, add more water to the dish to prevent the roast from drying out. After removing the roast from the oven, allow it to stand, covered, 10 minutes.

Reheat the sauce over low heat.

Transfer the roast and vegetables to a serving dish, and cover with 1 cup of the sauce. Garnish with sesame seeds. Serve immediately with additional sauce on the side.

*Yields 2½ cups sauce; serves 4-6*

*Note: This dish is delicious with steamed rice, tossed greens, and sliced oranges with ginger soy dressing and steamed snow peas. Add shiitake mushrooms as a garnish.*

*Teriyaki Beef with Toasted Sesame Seeds (recipe this page)*

# Condiments

top: Grilled Salmon with Green
Garlic Mayonnaise (recipes on
pages 127 and 152);
bottom: Rene's Spring Harvest Salad
(recipe on page 75)

# GREEN GARLIC MAYONNAISE

1 tablespoon white wine
  vinegar
1 tablespoon water
1 large egg, at room
  temperature
¼ cup tightly packed green
  basil leaves
1 tablespoon chopped fresh
  chives
1 teaspoon chopped fresh
  tarragon leaves
¼ cup chopped flat-leaf
  parsley
3 cloves garlic, halved
¼ teaspoon freshly ground
  white pepper
1 cup extra-virgin olive oil

*Green Garlic Mayonnaise can be served warm or at room temperature. It graces grilled fish, lamb, and steamed vegetables with a tangy combination of alliums and herbs. It does tend to be a bit thick and redolent with garlic, so eat it with good friends who enjoy the flavors as much as you do! (Photo on page 150.)*

In a blender, process the vinegar, water, egg, basil, chives, tarragon, parsley, garlic, and white pepper 10 seconds. Add 2 tablespoons of the oil and process another 10 seconds. With the motor running, slowly drizzle the remaining oil into the blender until all of the oil is absorbed and the mixture becomes a thick, green, creamy sauce. Serve immediately or transfer to an airtight container and refrigerate.

*Yields 1 cup*

*Note: This mayonnaise thickens well in the refrigerator and keeps 7-10 days.*

# EGGPLANT WITH GARLIC AND MINT

1 small eggplant
1 cup olive oil
½ teaspoon salt
1 teaspoon freshly ground
    white pepper
3 cloves garlic, minced
3 teaspoons dried mint

*Eggplant seasoned with garlic and mint can be eaten with pita bread and a glass of iced tea or added to a more complex meal. It complements Greek and southern Italian cuisine very well, and it keeps in the refrigerator for up to 3 weeks. It's an enjoyable treat for a large group of dinner guests because it can be made ahead and added to the table or buffet just before everyone is ready to dine. The eggplant tastes best when served at room temperature.*

Peel and cut the eggplant into ¼-inch-thick slices. Place the eggplant in a large bowl filled with 2 quarts water. Cover, allow the eggplant to soak 1 hour, then drain in a colander. Squeeze out any excess water.

In a blender or food processor, combine the oil, salt, pepper, garlic, and mint at low speed 30 seconds. Set aside.

In a large cast-iron skillet, gently cook the eggplant over medium heat about 1 minute on each side. Place the eggplant in an airtight plastic container, then drizzle the oil-garlic marinade over the slices. (There should be enough liquid to moisten and flavor the eggplant without soaking it.) Cover and refrigerate 3 days before serving.

*Serves 6-8*

# DRESSED KALAMATA

¼ cup extra-virgin olive oil

1 tablespoon chopped fresh
mint

½ teaspoon salt

½ teaspoon freshly ground
green peppercorns

1 tablespoon chopped garlic or
garlic chives

½ pound pitted kalamata
olives

4 ounces feta cheese, cut into
½-inch chunks or slices

½ cup chopped sweet red
onions

*O*lives are an ancient food, along with peppers, corn, and other
staples from the New World. Although California olives prevail
for most American palates, more exotic varieties now appear in super-
markets and delicatessens. While olives are 95% fat, they offer fat that
your body can use, lowering cholesterol and enhancing good health
with plenty of vitamin E. So try kalamata, gaeta, niçoise, or other
imported varieties. Olives are real food!*

In a small bowl, whisk together the
oil, mint, salt, green pepper, and
garlic. Drain the olives and place
them in a medium bowl. Spoon
half of the dressing over the olives.

Arrange the olives, cheese, and
onions on a serving dish. Drizzle
the remaining dressing over the
cheese and serve immediately.

*Serves 8-10*

*Note: This dish tastes best when
slightly cooler than room temperature.
If the feta cheese gets too warm, its
flavor overpowers the onions and
olives.*

# PRESERVED LEMONS

2 cups water
½ cup fresh lemon juice
4-5 lemons
⅓ cup kosher salt
¼ cup black or green olives
4 cloves garlic
4 bay leaves
1 tablespoon sugar

*P*reserved lemons make wonderful additions to pasta and risotto, as well as to soups and stews. They are frequently used in Moroccan dishes and add levity to grains, meats, and salads. In this recipe, the entire lemon can be cut and used. It seems a little silly to go through the process of preserving an entire lemon if only the flesh is used.

In a small saucepan, bring the water and lemon juice to a slow boil, then reduce the heat and simmer 5 minutes.

Wash and dry the lemons, making sure the skins are free of spots and nicks. Make a cross, about 1 inch deep, at the top of each lemon. Gently pull the lemons open and spoon some of the salt into each. Press the sides of the lemons closed.

Place the lemons, olives, garlic, bay leaves, and sugar in a sterilized quart jar. Pour the hot liquid over the lemons, then cover the jar with plastic wrap and screw the lid on tightly. Place the lemons in a cool, dark cabinet or pantry 5-7 days, turning the jar every other day to ensure that the liquid permeates all of the lemons. Serve at room temperature.

*Yields 1 quart*

*Note: Once opened, the jar of lemons can be refrigerated up to 2 weeks.*

# ORANGE-ONION SALSA

2 medium navel oranges
1 medium lemon
¼ cup chopped and pitted
  Spanish olives
¼ cup chopped bunching
  onions or scallions, green
  and white parts
2 tablespoons chopped yellow
  shallots
1 tablespoon chopped parsley
½ teaspoon honey
⅛ teaspoon ground ginger
⅛ teaspoon freshly ground
  green peppercorns, or
  minced chile

*T*he combination of citrus and ginger creates a fanciful salsa that adds zest to chilled shrimp, grilled chicken, and grilled beef. However, its possibilities as an appetizer seem limitless: You can serve it with jalapeños, hot pepper cheese, chive cream cheese, and bread sticks. You can also increase the level of heat by adding a chopped fresh serrano chile before serving.

Remove the outer peel and white pith from the oranges and lemon. Cut the oranges and lemon crosswise into ¼-inch slices, then cut the slices into smaller pieces of ½ inch to ¾ inch.

Place the oranges, lemons, olives, bunching onions, shallots, parsley, honey, ginger, and pepper in a small bowl. Gently stir the ingredients with a fork until blended. Serve immediately, or cover and refrigerate until you're ready to serve. Serve slightly cooler than room temperature.

*Yields 2 cups*

# TARRAGON VINAIGRETTE

½ teaspoon salt
1 tablespoon freshly ground
  green peppercorns
1 tablespoon white wine
  vinegar
4 tablespoons extra-virgin
  olive oil
1 tablespoon chopped fresh
  tarragon
2 tablespoons chopped fresh
  parsley
1 teaspoon fresh lemon thyme
½ teaspoon Dijon mustard

*Tarragon reigns here to provide a discreet tang to salads. This vinaigrette recipe doubles as a marinade for chicken and fish. The fresh young herbs that pop out of the ground in April make this a springtime favorite. It's also delicious over boiled baby potatoes, steamed carrots, green beans, and steamed fennel.*

In a small shaker jar, blend the salt, green pepper, vinegar, and oil. Shake 30 seconds. Add the tarragon, parsley, lemon thyme, and mustard, and shake another 30 seconds, or until the ingredients are blended. Serve immediately or refrigerate for future use.

*Yields ½ cup*

# PESTO PESTO

2 cups tightly packed
    Genovese basil
⅓ cup tightly packed lemon
    basil
2 cloves garlic
½ cup grated Parmagiano-
    Reggiano cheese
⅔ cup extra-virgin olive oil
½ teaspoon salt
½ teaspoon freshly ground
    green peppercorns
¼ cup toasted pine nuts,
    optional

*T*his classic pesto recipe adds the zest of fresh basil, garlic, and Parmesan to pasta, risotto, and sandwiches. It's also enjoyable warmed and served along with chunks of crusty bread and steamed vegetables. This recipe calls for a little lemon basil, but it is equally delicious when only green basil is used. When asked how I like pesto, I say, "On everything."

In a blender or food processor, combine the basils, garlic, and cheese until slightly chunky. With the motor running, gradually add the oil until completely blended. Transfer to a small bowl, then whisk in the salt and green pepper until well blended. If desired, add the pine nuts for a more intense pesto. Serve immediately.

*Yields 1 cup*

# JAMAICA JERK SAUCE

½ cup chopped scallions
⅓ cup lime juice
2 tablespoons dark molasses
3 tablespoons soy sauce
3 tablespoons chopped fresh
  ginger
4 cloves garlic, chopped
1 jalapeño chile, seeded and
  diced
1 serrano chile, seeded and
  diced
½ teaspoon ground cinnamon
¼ cup freshly ground nutmeg

*J*erk sauce resides in a class of its own. It serves as a basting sauce, hot sauce, and marinade all in one. The blend of spices and chiles offers a flavor sensation that cannot be duplicated for grilled meat, shrimp and other seafood, and poultry. This recipe doubles easily, providing plenty of zest for that last big barbecue at the end of summer.

In a blender or food processor, place the scallions, lime juice, molasses, soy sauce, ginger, garlic, chiles, cinnamon, and nutmeg. Pulse 10-15 seconds, or until well blended. Transfer the sauce to a small container. Serve immediately or cover and refrigerate.

*Yields 1 cup*

# CHILE-ONION VINAIGRETTE AND MARINADE

⅓ cup white wine vinegar
2 tablespoons lime juice
⅔ cup extra-virgin olive oil
¼ cup chopped red Spanish
  onions
1 teaspoon chopped fresh
  *epazote*
1-2 canned chipotle chiles in
  adobo sauce
1-2 tablespoons adobo sauce
½ teaspoon salt

*This is a great marinade for grilled onions, eggplant, elephant garlic, peppers, and summer squash. You can also try it with kabobs of cubed chicken breast, shrimp, and scallions. As a vinaigrette, use it on a salad of mixed greens, green beans, and corn. This recipe doubles easily.*

In a blender, mix the vinegar, lime juice, and oil 5 seconds. Add the onions, *epazote*, chiles, adobo sauce, and salt, and blend 3-5 seconds. Use immediately or transfer to an airtight container and refrigerate.

*Yields 1 cup*

*Note: This marinade keeps well in the refrigerator 2-3 weeks.*

# RED BELL AND ONION
# BARBECUE SAUCE

24 large ripe plum tomatoes,
    seeded and chopped
1 cup chopped sweet Spanish
    onions
1 cup chopped white globe
    onions
½ cup chopped garlic
2 cups seeded and chopped
    red bell peppers
2 tablespoons dried onion
    flakes
1½-2 tablespoons crushed red
    pepper
1 cup brown sugar
½ cup unsulphured molasses
2 tablespoons wheat-free
    tamari sauce
1 teaspoon dried mustard
1 tablespoon paprika
1 tablespoon salt
1 cup white distilled vinegar

*B*arbecue sauce takes a little time to cook and process, but the rewards are well worth the work during the chill of winter. Make a double batch, and keep the harvest alive long after the first snowfall.

In a large stockpot, cook the tomatoes, onions, garlic, and bell peppers 30 minutes over medium heat. Add the onion flakes, red pepper, brown sugar, molasses, tamari, mustard, paprika, salt, and vinegar, and cook another 30-40 minutes, stirring occasionally to prevent the mixture from sticking.

Remove the pot from the heat and allow the mixture to cool 15-20 minutes. Transfer to a blender or food processor, and blend at high speed 5-10 seconds, depending on how chunky or smooth you like your barbecue sauce. Place the sauce in an airtight container and refrigerate 24 hours before serving.

If you want to can some of the sauce, return the sauce to the stockpot and bring it to a boil. Pour into hot, sterilized jars. Screw the lids and rings tightly on the jars, then process in a boiling-water bath or pressure canner, following the processing time for your altitude. Remove the jars from the water, and let stand in a draft-free area until the lids have popped. Transfer to a cool shelf in your pantry.

*Yields 2½ pints*

*Note: This sauce retains its color and flavor in the pantry 6-10 months.*

# METRIC CONVERSIONS

## Dry Weights

| U.S. Measurements | Metric Equivalents |
|---|---|
| ¼ ounce | 7 grams |
| ⅓ ounce | 10 grams |
| ½ ounce | 14 grams |
| 1 ounce | 28 grams |
| 1½ ounces | 42 grams |
| 1¾ ounces | 50 grams |
| 2 ounces | 57 grams |
| 3 ounces | 85 grams |
| 3½ ounces | 100 grams |
| 4 ounces (¼ pound) | 114 grams |
| 6 ounces | 170 grams |
| 8 ounces (½ pound) | 227 grams |
| 9 ounces | 250 grams |
| 16 ounces (1 pound) | 464 grams |

## Liquid Weights

| U.S. Measurements | Metric Equivalents |
|---|---|
| ¼ teaspoon | 1.23 ml |
| ½ teaspoon | 2.5 ml |
| ¾ teaspoon | 3.7 ml |
| 1 teaspoon | 5 ml |
| 1 dessertspoon | 10 ml |
| 1 tablespoon (3 teaspoons) | 15 ml |
| 2 tablespoons (1 ounce) | 30 ml |
| ¼ cup | 60 ml |
| ⅓ cup | 80 ml |
| ½ cup | 120 ml |
| ⅔ cup | 160 ml |
| ¾ cup | 180 ml |
| 1 cup (8 ounces) | 240 ml |
| 2 cups (1 pint) | 480 ml |
| 3 cups | 720 ml |
| 4 cups (1 quart) | 1 liter |
| 4 quarts (1 gallon) | 3¾ liters |

## Length

| U.S. Measurements | Metric Equivalents |
|---|---|
| ⅛ inch | 3 mm |
| ¼ inch | 6 mm |
| ⅜ inch | 1 cm |
| ½ inch | 1.2 cm |
| 1 inch | 2.5 cm |
| ¾ inch | 2 cm |
| 1¼ inches | 3.1 cm |
| 1½ inches | 3.7 cm |
| 2 inches | 5 cm |
| 3 inches | 7.5 cm |
| 4 inches | 10 cm |
| 5 inches | 12.5 cm |

## Temperatures

| Fahrenheit | Celsius (Centigrade) |
|---|---|
| 32°F (water freezes) | 0°C |
| 200°F | 95°C |
| 212°F (water boils) | 100°C |
| 250°F | 120°C |
| 275°F | 135°C |
| 300°F (slow oven) | 150°C |
| 325°F | 160°C |
| 350°F (moderate oven) | 175°C |
| 375°F | 190°C |
| 400°F (hot oven) | 205°C |
| 425°F | 220°C |
| 450°F (very hot oven) | 230°C |
| 475°F | 245°C |
| 500°F (extremely hot oven) | 260°C |

# SOURCES

**Asgrow Seed Company**
1905 Lirio Avenue
Saticoy, CA 93007-4206
Phone: (805) 647-5912
Fax: (805) 647-3694
*Seed supplier to commercial growers. Has an extensive list of varieties and offers comprehensive information about onion culture management.*

**Bland Farms**
Highway 169, Box 506
Glennville, GA 30453
Phone: (912) 654-2723
*Grower, packer, shipper, and processor of Vidalia onions. Offers exceptional service. Mail order, cookbook, and free catalog available.*

**Cheese Importers**
33 South Pratt Parkway
Longmont, CO 80501
Phone: (303) 443-4444
Fax: (303) 443-4492
*Wholesaler specializing in cheeses, oils, vinegars, and specialty items such as textiles and kitchenware from all over the world.*

**Columbia Publishing**
P.O. Box 9036
Yakima, WA 98909-0036
Phone: (509) 248-2452
Fax: (509) 248-4056
*Publisher of* Onion World, *which appears eight times per year. This periodical is the voice of the onion industry and addresses topics of interest to industry participants.*

**George W. Park Seed Company**
Cokesbury Road
Greenwood, SC 29467-0001
Phone: (800) 845-3369
Fax: (864) 941-4206
*Seed garden supplier for a wide variety of vegetables and fruits. Free catalog.*

**Filaree Farm**
182 Conconully Highway
Okanogan, WA 98840
Phone: (509) 422-6940
*Mail-order supplier of more than 125 strains of early-season, midseason, and late-season garlic. Varieties include an array of tried-and-true hardneck and softneck garlic as well as more exotic types. The catalog includes helpful information about garlic culture, management, and flavor.*

**Joe's Vegetables**
P.O. Box 2494
Hollister, CA 95024
Phone: (408) 636-3224
Fax: (408) 636-3226
*Organic wholesaler of exceptional alliums and capsicums. Processing plants in Oregon dehydrate, purée, freeze, brine, and fresh-process onions, garlic, bell peppers, chiles, and other vegetables.*

**Johnny's Selected Seeds**
Foss Hill Road
Albion, ME 04910-9731
Phone: (207) 437-4301
Fax: (207) 437-4301
*An all-purpose garden supplier that offers high-quality seeds for vegetables, flowers (including edible flowers), and herbs. Free catalog.*

**Le Jardin du Gourmet**
P.O. Box 75
St. Johnsbury Center, VT 05863-0075
Phone: (800) 659-1446
Fax: (802) 748-9592
*A superior supplier of shallots, onions, mushrooms, and seeds for a variety of herbs and vegetables.*

**Nichols Garden Nursery**
1190 North Pacific Highway
Albany, OR 97321-4580
Phone: (541) 928-9280
Fax: (541) 967-8406
*A family-owned seed company. The free mail-order catalog contains a wide variety of garden seeds, as well as selected plants, bulbs, and tubers.*

**Pope Produce**
3097 Road T
Wiggins, CO 80654
Phone: (970) 483-7839
Fax: (970) 483-7211
*Supplier of quality peppers and onions, other vegetables, and melons.*

**Sandy Mush Nursery**
Rt. 2, Surrett Cove Rd.
Leicester, NC 28748
Phone: (704) 683-2014
*Seed and plant supplier with a comprehensive array of herbs and gourmet vegetables.*

**Shepherd's Garden Seeds**
30 Irene St.
Torrington, CT 06790-6627
Phone: (408) 335-6910
*Mail-order seed supplier of vegetables, flowers, and herbs. Free catalog.*

**Seeds of Change**
P.O. Box 15700
Santa Fe, NM 87506-5700
Phone: (888) 762-7333
Fax: (888) 329-4762
*Mail-order supplier of organic seeds. Free catalog includes helpful information about genetic variability and biodiversity in agricultural crops.*

**The Cook's Garden**
P.O. Box 535
Londonderry, VT 05148
Phone: (800) 457-9703
Fax: (800) 457-9705
*Mail-order supplier of outstanding organic seeds and plants. Free catalog also includes miscellaneous garden tools and supplies.*

**University of Hawaii**
**Department of Horticulture**
3190 Maile Way, Room 112
Honolulu, HI 96822-2279
*Provides a variety of seeds through mail order and offers sturdy strains of Japanese scallions.*

**W. Atlee Burpee**
300 Park Avenue
Warminster, PA 18974
Phone: (215) 674-4900
Fax: (215) 674-4170
*Mail-order seed supplier of vegetables, flowers, and herbs. The free catalog also includes gardener's tools.*

# BIBLIOGRAPHY

Bothwell, Jean. *Onions without Tears*. New York: Hastings House, 1950.

Casas, Penelope. *Delicioso!* New York: Alfred A. Knopf, 1996.

Child, Julia, Louisette Bertolle, and Simone Beck. *Mastering the Art of French Cooking, vol. 1.* New York: Alfred A. Knopf, 1961.

Chioffi, Nancy, and Gretchen Mead. *Keeping the Harvest*. Pownal, Vt.: Storey Communications, 1994.

Curry, S. J., Brother Rick. *The Secrets of Jesuit Breadmaking*. New York: HarperCollins, 1995.

Foster, Steven. *Herbal Renaissance*. Salt Lake City: Gibbs-Smith, 1997.

Engeland, Ron L. *Growing Great Garlic*. Okanogan, Wash.: Filaree Productions, 1996.

Gordon, Leslie. *A Country Herbal*. New York: Mayflower Books, 1980.

Griffith, Fred, and Linda Griffith. *Onions, Onions, Onions*. Shelburne, Vt.: Chapters Publishing Ltd., 1994.

Harris, Lloyd J. *The Book of Garlic*. Menlo Park, Calif.: Addison-Wesley, 1979.

Hausman, Patricia, and Judith Benn Hurley. *The Healing Foods*. Emmaus, Pa.: Rodale Press, 1989.

Hupping, Carol, and the staff at the Rodale Cooking Center. *Stocking Up*. New York: Simon & Schuster, 1986.

Kasper, Lynne Rossetto. *The Splendid Table*. New York: William Morrow & Company, 1991.

Kershner, Ruth. *Greek Cooking*. New York: Weathervane Books, 1977.

Mendelsohn, Oscar A. *A Salute to Onions*. New York: Hawthorn Books, 1965.

Murphy, Martha Watson. *A New England Fish Tale*. New York: Henry Holt and Company, 1997.

Ogden, Shepherd, and Ellen Ogden. *The Cook's Garden*. Emmaus, Pa.: Rodale Press, 1989.

Ogden, Shepherd. *Step By Step Organic Vegetable Gardening*. New York: HarperCollins, 1992.

Paston-Williams, Sara. *The Art of Dining*. Oxford, England: Past Times, 1996.

Phillips, Roger, and Rix Martyn. *The Random House Book of Vegetables*. New York: Random House, 1993.

Roberts-Dominguez, Jan. *The Onion Book*. New York: Doubleday, 1996.

Rupp, Rebecca. *Blue Corn & Square Tomatoes*. Pownal, Vt.: Storey Communications, 1987.

Swahn, J. O. *The Lore of Spices*. New York: Crescent Books, 1991.

Trager, James. *The Food Chronology*. New York: Henry Holt and Company, 1995.

Wolfert, Paula. *Couscous and Other Good Food from Morocco*. New York: Harper & Row, 1983.

# PHOTO CREDITS

## COVER
Boyd Hagen

## THE GENUS *ALLIUM*
pg. 5: David Cavagnaro
pgs. 6, 10, 11: Corbis-Bettmann
pg. 7: Scott Vlaun
pgs. 9, 12: Derek Fell
pg. 13: The Granger Collection, New York

## A GALLERY OF ALLIUMS
pg. 15: Mick Hales
pgs. 18 (right), 24, 25, 29 (right), 30, 31 (top left, top middle, top right), 32 (top right), 33 (top left): David Cavagnaro
pgs. 18 (left), 19, 33 (top middle, top right): Scott Vlaun
pgs. 20, 23 (left), 28 (right): W. Atlee Burpee & Co.
pg. 21 (left): Bland Farms
pgs. 21 (right), 22 (top left), 23 (right), 28 (left): Derek Fell
pg. 22 (top right, bottom): courtesy of Johnny's Selected Seeds, Albion, Maine
pg. 26: Scott Phillips
pg. 27: Boyd Hagen
pgs. 29 (left), 31 (bottom), 32 (top left): photography by Benko Photographics
pg. 32 (bottom): courtesy of The Cook's Garden

## HARVESTING AND STORING
pgs. 35, 36, 37, 38 (left): David Cavagnaro
pg. 38 (right): Derek Fell
pgs. 39, 40: photography by Benko Photographics

## COOKING AND BAKING
pg. 43: David Cavagnaro
pgs. 44, 45, 46, 47, 48, 49, 50: photography by Benko Photographics

## RECIPES
pgs. 54, 59, 62, 67, 72, 77, 80, 85, 88, 90, 94, 99, 102, 104, 109, 112, 118, 123, 130, 135, 141, 146, 149, 150: Boyd Hagen

# INDEX

BOOK PUBLISHER: Jim Childs

ASSOCIATE PUBLISHER: Helen Albert

EDITORIAL ASSISTANT: Cherilyn DeVries


EDITOR: Diane Sinitsky

DESIGNER: Jodie Delohery

LAYOUT ARTIST: Michael Mandarano

ILLUSTRATOR:  Rosalie Vaccaro


RECIPE TESTER: Connie Welch

ART DIRECTOR FOR FOOD PHOTOGRAPHY: Henry Roth

FOOD STYLIST: Abigail Johnson Dodge

PROP STYLIST: Sheila F. Shulman
Props supplied by Pier One, Pottery Barn, Kaplan and Associates


TYPEFACE: Berling

PAPER: 70-lb. Somerset Gloss

PRINTER: R. R. Donnelley, Willard, Ohio